Security from Identity Theft

Book Two

Like a Rock

with Study Guide

Sid Huston

CrownScepter316

Identity, Authority
& the Good News

Sid Huston Media

First Printing January 2008
©2007 Sid Huston, Colorado Springs, CO
All Rights Reserved

Pastoral teaching in this book is the personal experience of the author. Neither evaluation, criticism or judgment is implied nor written. Author makes no claim as a psychotherapist or medical practitioner of any kind.

Published by
Little Blue Barn
2814 East Woodmen Road
Colorado Springs, CO 80920
719-266-0437 / 800-266-0999
my2bits@earthlink.net
www.mothershousepublishing.com

Layout by Jacqueline Haag
Printed and bound in Colorado Springs, CO

Little Blue Barn is an imprint of Mother's House Publishing, Colorado Springs CO

Made in the United States of America
ISBN-10: 0-9797144-1-9
ISBN-13: 978-0-9797144-1-2

To schedule Sid for speaking, contact him at:Sidhuston@msn.com

I gladly dedicate this book to my dad, Sam Huston. Goodness and mercy have gone before me because he has been "like a rock." In 1976 I was attending Kearney State College and I had accumulated a glove-box full of parking tickets. The rumor around campus was that the new parking lots that were being built were being financed by these parking tickets. With all this new construction going on it was really difficult to find a place to hide my car, I guess the campus cops didn't have a problem finding it.

The day came when I faced the fact that these tickets had to be paid for, so I reluctantly worked up the gumption and walked to the parking ticket office. I stood in line; this was not a happy place. When I faced the lady behind the window she smiled and asked, "Are you from Grand Island?" I answered, yes I am. She then asked, "Is your dad Sam Huston?" I answered yes. And then I witnessed goodness and mercy, she tore up those tickets. And then she said, "There was a time when I needed some help and your dad helped me out, I am happy to return the favor."

If you think she was happy, I was elated, and relieved. And once again humbled by the blessing my Heavenly father gave me when he chose to make my dad my "Earthly father." Dad gets a kick out of calling and saying this is your "Earthly Father" speaking. So I must say thanks to my two dads, my Heavenly Father and my "Earthly Father," and I dedicate this book to my dad by saying: it has been a privilege to be Sam Huston's son. Thank you, God, for giving me a Godly Dad.

Like a Rock

Psalm 18:1-3

"I love you. O Lord, my strength. The Lord is my rock, my fortress and my deliverer. My God is my rock, in whom I take refuge. He is my shield and the horn of salvation, my stronghold. I call to the Lord, who is worthy of praise."

Psalm 95: 1-3

"Come, let us sing for joy to the LORD; let us shout aloud to the Rock of our Salvation. Let us come before him with thanksgiving and extol him with music and joy. For the LORD is the Great God, the Great King above all gods."

Table of Contents

SECTION ONE: KNOW IT!.. 1

Chapter 1 CAN'T STANDS NO MORE 5

Chapter 2 THE JOSEPH STORY 15

Chapter 3 DILUTED MAN 27

Chapter 4 BE A MENORAH 39

SECTION TWO: NAME IT!.. 49

Chapter 5 LIKE A ROCK STAR...51

Chapter 6 GREAT FAKE OUTS...65

Chapter 7 GOD'S JEHOVAH NAMES 75

Chapter 8 RESPECT OUR ROOT 87

Chapter 9 OWN YOUR OWN GOOD NAME 97

SECTION THREE: ENGRAVE IT! 109

Chapter 10 BADGES, LANYARDS, UNIFORMS, AND TRAMP STAMPS..111

Chapter 11 THE MARK...123

Chapter 12 COVENANT IDENTITY 131

Chapter 13 IDENTITY IN COMMUNION 143

SECTION FOUR: ROCK IT!.. 151

Chapter 14 THE ATTRIBUTES OF GOD "ROCK" OUR IDENTITY 155

Chapter 15 GOD'S PURPOSES FOR HIS LAWS...165

Chapter 16 GOD'S FEASTS 179

Chapter 17 BLUE DEVILED...197

SECURITY FROM IDENTITY THEFT STUDY GUIDES & DISCUSSION QUESTIONS FOR SMALL GROUPS............. 205

Section One:
KNOW IT!

Now this is eternal life; that they may know you, the only true God, and Jesus Christ, whom you have sent.
John 17:3

At each section division we will be introduced to an identity security concept from a physical or financial standpoint. Each of these concepts has important applications with regards to finances, reputations, and valuable information. Our first concept is "Access Control."

Access Control: In the physical realm, access control is the ability to restrict entrance into an area, a building, or a room. This can be accomplished by stationing a guard, a bouncer, or a receptionist. In a mechanical way, access can be controlled by locks and keys, or with the use of technology and some kind of scan device, or card access system.

To protect our computers we need to employ access control. This includes authentication, encryption and authorization (Terms we will look at in the next section divisions). To accomplish this type of guardianship on our computers, we can use physical apparatus like biometric scans[1], metal locks, hidden parts, digital signatures, encryption, social barriers, and automated monitoring

---

[1] Biometric scans turn fingerprint, facial, and hand geometries into "biotopes" that can be used to verify a person's identity for a financial transaction.

systems. Our objective here is to always make sure that the only people who have access to our computer are the ones we want to have it. In other words, only the people who have the identities that we have prequalified. Each user must then be able to verify that they have the proper user I.D. Only by having Access Control can we be assured of our security from identity theft.

 __Access Control Systems__ provide us with the following security measures.

- *Identification and Authentication, so we can know who can log on to the computer system, and control who has this access.*
- *We want to determine and limit what a person/subject can do while on our computer. Therefore, we want to limit access to other sites and information (Like in a corporate building, we might not want everyone to have access to the fifth floor.)*
- *We want anyone who uses our computer system to be accountable and held responsible for their actions. Therefore their time on the computer will be recorded.*

 This section is called "Know-it!"

From a spiritual standpoint we do not want the Identity Thief or any of his accomplices to have access to our hearts and our relationships, so we must control his access. The way we do this is to have our identity secured by Authority, Authentication, and Encryption; only by employing these processes in a spiritual way can we truly be secure and

"Know-It!" By developing a grasp of these principles you can have security from identity theft.

 *Something to think about: How does our access to the very Throne of Grace make it possible for our lives to be positively transformed? Think about the power of prayer and the confidence God's presence gives us (Hebrews 4:14-16).*

Chapter 1
CAN'T STANDS NO MORE

Matthew Chapter 7

The Saturday morning cartoons feature my hero, "Popeye the Sailor Man." I don't know why I have always been smitten by this crusty old one-eyed swab, but I am. Maybe it is his "can-do" attitude, bulging forearms with tattoos of anchors, and an anger problem to which I can relate.

I liked his famous jingle—it is an identity statement! "I yam what I yam and that's all I yam." Yet when his arch rival, Bluto, would try and steal away his sweetie, Olive Oyl, Popeye's arms would flex and swing, his corn-cob pipe would rise-up, and from the side of his mouth Popeye would utter with unction, "I've had all I can stands and I can't stands no more." Then he would pop open a can of spinach and gulp it down as if he had just ingested a can of "I am going to whoop your you-know-what."

The Popeye jingle would play, "I am strong to the finish because I eat me spinach," and there I was, in my pajamas, excited to see Popeye pummel Bluto. And there was Olive Oyl, looking so impressed, fluttering her eyelids, her heart twitterpating. Once again, this old sailor saved the day and saved his sweetie. Can you hear her swoon for him? Can you see me cheering him on?

Popeye was "like a rock" when it came to avenging his Olive Oyl, and so was Karen Lodrick, who endured six months of hell because her identity had been stolen. She had toiled and suffered to try and regain her identity and restore her financial status. Then, one eventful morning, she was standing in line at Starbucks getting a coffee when she saw the woman who had run off with her identity. In this moment, Karen essentially said, "I've had all I can stands and I can't stands no more." Karen, who weighs no more than 110 pounds, became like the Rock of Gibraltar and was determined to crush her offender. In a few moments she would begin tracking the thief who stole her identity through the streets of San Francisco. This was a thriller of a chase, one made for the silver screen.

In 2006 there were 8.4 million victims of identity fraud, but there is only one story like Karen Lodrick's. I pronounce her name "like a rock." In the six months she suffered with a lost identity, Karen watched her bank account dwindle and her credit destroyed. Because of this constant distraction, she lost over thirty thousand dollars in her consulting business. She had a never-ending struggle with her bank and credit agencies, and received very little help from them. No one person ever took up her cause; she felt like she was always being passed off to another incompetent and uncaring employee. Yet her thief had applied for and received new credit cards and was *ka-ching, ka-ching, ka-chinging* away while shopping at all the exclusive stores. Putting an end to this fraud was now Karen's full-time job.

The people at the bank showed Karen a picture of the woman who was photographed by a security camera while she was emptying Karen's bank account. Karen wasn't about to forget the expensive brown suede coat in which this woman was pictured. She studied this picture as a CSI agent would examine the evidence of a crime scene.

Karen received a break in her case when a branch location of her bank called her to tell her that she had accidentally left her driver's license at the teller's window. Karen knew this wasn't the bank location she frequented, so she went early the next day to pick it up. This was April twenty-fourth, and she got there so early that the bank wasn't yet open, so she ventured into Starbucks for a coffee. Karen ordered her coffee, turned while she waited for it to be prepared, and there it was: the coat in the picture. The distinctive and expensive brown suede coat, folded over the arm of the woman right behind her. She had carefully analyzed this coat in the picture; she knew the stitching, the fir trim, and the cuffs. This woman was her Identity Thief; this is the woman who had been living off of her, who had been ripping her off for these last six months.

Mike Weiss, who used to write for the *San Francisco Chronicle*, originally told this story, and when he came to this scene my mind went wild with questions: How would Karen verify this woman's identity? Would she eavesdrop on the woman's conversations? Would she try to engage her in some small talk? Or would she steal her purse? What she did do was call 911.

Karen Lodrick observed that this woman, whose real name is Maria Nelson, seemed to be inconsistent. She noticed that Maria had really expensive clothes, a Prada Bag, and Gucci glasses, but she also had bad teeth and looked rather unkept, like she hadn't bathed for several days. Karen, who once stood before crowds as a stand-up comic, said, "I thought, 'Here you are buying Prada on my dime, go get your teeth fixed.'" I imagine this Starbucks experience to be a bit of a time warp, with Karen viewing Maria and thinking, "How do you solve a problem like Maria?"

When Maria got up to leave this Starbucks, little Karen, who is only five-foot-two and one hundred and ten pounds, acted like Popeye when he had just downed a can of spinach, and said, "I can't stands no more." The chase was on.

There was great tension in Karen's every step, but the thoughts of her six months of being tortured by Maria motivated her to hard pursuit. Even though Maria had made Karen's life miserable and scary, Karen was totally committed not to let Maria out of her sight. While trailing Maria, Karen kept the 911 operator up to speed about her locations.

While hot on Maria's heals, Karen experienced a thud in her gut. As she walked over a San Francisco hill and turned a corner, Maria vanished. In a few moments of desperate scanning, Karen caught a glimpse of Maria the thief catching her breath in the entry way of an apartment building.

Having been sighted, Maria bolted for a cab, but Karen Lodrick remained "rock-like," went right up to the cabbie, and told him, "911 is on the phone—please don't drive away. I think she is stealing my identity." The driver cooperated; he lifted his hands from the steering wheel.

Maria jumped from the cab and yelled back, "Stop following me, you are scaring me."

Karen said, "I'm scared, too; let's just wait for the police and we can straighten this out."

Maria shouted back, "I can't, I am on probation." Her fear of being caught had made her heart race faster, and her steps quickened. Karen, while on the beat, took to her cell phone and relayed this information to the 911 operator while hustling through a grocery store. Karen, alert like a shortstop, picked up some of the discarded items Maria was flinging from her Prada purse. From a grocery cart she snatched her wallet.

Maria hopped onto a bus for a short ride, and then they were beating their feet on the streets again. Karen's heart sank again in disappointment as she lost Maria in a Walgreens parking lot. She dialed the 911 operator and frantically begged for a police officer to come before it was too late. In a minute Officer Rickey Terrell arrived, a full forty-five minutes after the chase had commenced. Officer Terrell found Maria squatting behind a car sucking on a cigarette. Karen, every bit "like a rock," laughed at Maria and impulsively said, "You idiot, you should have run."

A month and two weeks later, on June sixth, Maria was in front of Superior Judge Harold Kahn's court to plead guilty to one felony count of fraudulently using another person's identity. Judge Kahn sentenced her to the forty-four days she had served since the day she was caught in the chase.

Still like a rock, Karen Lodrick issued a statement of her dissatisfaction with this ruling. She said, "I can't believe it. I went through six months of hell, and she is going to get probation? She was on probation when she victimized me. Obviously probation's not helping."

Maria was not humble in this court room; she smirked and waved at Karen as she sported her orange, jail-issued jumpsuit. Judge Kahn reprimanded her for this attitude and tacked on psychological and drug counseling to the sentence. Maria also found out that she was facing more fraud charges from another county.

When Karen picked up the driver's license at the bank, she found it to be a near-perfect forgery. It even came with a hologram of the California seal emblazoned on it. It had Karen's name on it, but it adorned Maria's picture. It is sad to note that these holograms that are meant to prevent identity theft can be purchased by fraudsters from supposedly legitimate companies—money talks.

From the wallet she picked up in the grocery cart, Karen found credit cards, a debit card, and a Social Security card all in her name.

This story eventually got untangled like a messed-up string of Christmas lights. Karen found out that her postal carrier reported that the master keys to the neighborhood's mailboxes and been stolen. Karen believes that Maria rifled through the mail and found her Social Security number and personal identification numbers from a certificate of deposit statement in her mail. With this information, Maria was able to order several new credit cards to be sent to her in Karen's name. It is a very convenient form of theft.

Maria then lived large on Karen's stolen identity. In her first three days with Karen's credit cards and fabricated driver's license, she binged on nine thousand dollars' worth of big spending. Maria gobbled up stuff like a bulimic eater gobbles food. She bought jewelry, clothing, accessories, groceries, computers, cigarettes, and booze. Perhaps she needed the booze to mask her guilty feelings.

The police who worked the case were so impressed with Karen Lodrick that they asked her to join their force. They stated that she had the natural instincts of a cop and that she would make a great detective. Though flattered, Karen turned down this invitation to work in the arena of identity theft prevention. Yet, in reality, none of us can refuse to work in this arena. Karen lived through six months of hell because her financial accounts were raided the way pirates loot ships and set them on fire.

But there is much more to identity theft than threats to our financial security; our spiritual security is threatened every day by the Identity Thief. We need to be "like a rock" in this daily battle.

Jesus Christ, in His classic Sermon on the Mount, concludes His teaching in Matthew chapter seven with insights into the Identity Thief, identity thieves, strategies for theft, and how we can be established on the rock so that we can be secure from identity theft. In Matthew 7:15 He said, "Watch out for false prophets, they come to you in sheep's clothing, but inwardly they are ferocious wolves." Jesus lets us know that the identity thieves disguise their identity so that they look like good and upstanding people. If they looked vicious and devious, we wouldn't give them the time of day.

The Apostle Paul writes that the Devil masquerades as an "angel of light," (2 Cor. 11:14). and he warns us to be wise and realize that these false servants will look righteous, and they will fit in like chameleons. The Identity Thief himself doesn't wear a red devil costume complete with pointy ears, a tail, and a pitchfork. This thief and his minions will fit right in; they will look and act like the person you want to bring home to meet your mom. But, if you look in his wallet, you just might find your own driver's license, Social Security card, and credit cards with perfect holograms. These thieves lack conscience and feed off of your life.

So, even though he looks to be as bright and fresh as a Colorado morning, he is the prince of darkness, and he will bring a destructive funnel cloud into your home if you let him. When he knocks on your door, you will see a smile. He will probably be polite, and you will be drawn to him. This is his *modis operandi*; it is his design to get you to drop your guard so you will give him access into your life and your home to murder your identity and the identities of those you love.

Jesus helps us learn to discern this real enemy of our souls when he says, "By their fruit you will recognize them. Do people pick grapes from thorn bushes, or figs from thistles? Likewise every good tree bears good fruit, but a bad tree bears bad fruit. A good tree cannot bear bad fruit, and a bad tree can not bear good fruit. Every tree that does not bear good fruit is cut down and thrown into the fire. Thus by their fruits you will recognize them" (Matt. 7:16-20)

There is an old adage that states, "You can't tell a book by its cover." We all know that a book can have a an attractive cover on the outside, and yet its pages can be filled with profanity, pornography, and all forms of mental and moral pollution. Likewise, we have all been pleasantly surprised by the plain-covered book that is chock full of life-giving and uplifting words. Our culture has been duped by this emphasis on the cover time and time again. We need to learn to discern the pages and study the content to see if it's wholesome.

It is interesting to me to reflect on Matthew 7:1 (same chapter), which says, "Do not judge, or you to will be judged." I believe the Identity Thief has caused this passage to become popular in circles hostile to God and be misused. Many times I have heard people say "judge not," as if to say it is not your job to evaluate someone's character, reliance on truth, and citizenship. The devil tries to get us to drop our guard, and open our lives to people of disrepute who have connections to the Identity Thief.

What Jesus means by His exhortation not to judge is don't be the person who says to this one, "You are going to heaven," and to another, "You are going to hell." That is not our role; only God is the true Judge in that sense of the word. He also wants us to quit judging others from a self-righteous standpoint and give up the play acting which is hypocrisy. What He wants from us is transparency and a humble stance towards others.

As we follow this chapter's progression we see His admonition to discern a person's character, and this really does require honest thinking and serious evaluation. Yes, we are called to evaluate people and make value judgments. Jesus tells us something that at first glance appears to be unthinkable when He says, "Do not give to dogs what is sacred; do not throw your pearls to pigs. If you do, they may trample them under their feet, and then turn and tear you to pieces" (Matt. 7:6). He is telling us to be like a rock and learn to pick out the pigs and the dogs in our world. We don't give them access to our hearts and our valuable identity information because, like pigs and dogs, they will devour us.

In verses 16-20, Jesus gives us another approach to evaluating the influences in our lives. He moves from pigs and dogs to good trees and bad trees—real-life pictures with which we are all familiar. He gives us a very practical way to distinguish the good trees from the bad. Basically, He tells us to inspect the fruit—go to the orchard, take a good look at the trees, and evaluate the fruit to see if it is good or bad. If the tree looks good but it has no fruit, you know that this tree is all show and no go. If the tree has pretty branches, deep green leaves, and well-shaped fruit, yet the fruit is filled with worms and covered in mold, it is bad. Throw it out.

On the other hand, there are some old and wind-beaten trees that have some of the most luscious and sweet fruit hanging from their branches. Go ahead, pick this fruit; it is good, good for you, and the kind of influence God wants in our lives.

Jesus says things in His own unique way. If a tree is good, so is its fruit. If a tree is a bad, so is its fruit. You can tell a good tree by its fruit. This is why He is so right when He says you can tell a good tree by its fruit. To make this clear teaching even more clear, we know that Jesus is talking about people—the nature and character of people.

If a person looks good, but in their wake is ruined relationships and abuse, you are probably looking at a bad-tree type of person. But if the person you are looking at might be missing a few branches, but their lives are characterized by Godly character, good decisions, and life-giving associations, you are probably looking at a good person. And if you find genuine love, the basis for the "fruit of the Spirit," (Gal. 5:22-23).[2] it results in true joy and creates peace in hearts and minds. If this fruit of the Spirit is prevalent, you are probably looking at a good tree. And if this person lives this way, you will observe life-giving sprouts blossoming all around him. I am talking about changed lives; a good tree naturally bears good fruit, and in the life of a mature believer in Jesus we see this clearly in this person's character and in those he converts. A good tree of a person will reproduce as the seed of the Word of God will be released from the good tree person, and naturally new trees will be born again.

Jesus, who is the Lord of love and life, says a hard word to the bad trees in the world, "Every tree that does not bear good fruit is cut down and thrown into the fire. Thus by their fruit you will recognize them" (Matt. 7:19). This will be the end of the Identity Thief and all of the people and demons who follow his deceptive ways.

The Lord Jesus takes this explanation to an even deeper level when He says, "Not everyone who says to me 'Lord, Lord' will enter the kingdom of heaven, but only he who does the will of my Father who is in heaven. Many will say to me on that day, 'Lord, Lord, did we not prophesy in your name, and in your name drive out demons and perform many miracles?' Then I will tell them plainly, 'I never knew you. Away from me, you evil doers!'" (Matt. 7:20-23). What He is saying is that, just like Maria did many things in Karen's identity, there will be bad people who will look so good that we might think—

---

[2] See Appendix #1 on page 219.

and they might think—they are in the Lord, but they are not; they are bad trees. Think about all the religious people in Jesus' day, and even today. They look so pious and even "do good things," but in reality they are spiritually dead and have a sinister influence on the world.

Jesus concludes this famous sermon with a teaching about himself. He does a compare and contrast segment and puts His identity up against the identity of the Identity Thief. He has already told us about the Identity Thief's methods, message, and the mess in which he puts his followers, and now He shows us a stark comparison.

He represents Himself as the Rock, the rock that can provide us with security from identity theft. David wrote a Psalm that God's children have loved for centuries. In Psalm 18:1-3 he said, "I love you O LORD, my strength. The LORD is my rock, my fortress and my deliverer; my god is my rock, in whom I take refuge. He is my shield and the horn of my salvation, my stronghold. I call to the LORD, who is worthy of praise, and I am saved from my enemies."

I believe when Jesus concludes this Sermon on the Mount He gives all of us the way to overcome the Identity Thief by establishing our lives on Him who is the rock—our rock, our fortress, refuge, and deliverer. He wants to be our shield and save us from being ripped off. He says:

> Therefore everyone who hears these words of mine and puts them into practice is like a wise man who built his house on the rock. The rain came down, the streams rose, and the winds blew and beat against the house. Yet it did not fall, because it had its foundation on the rock. But everyone who hears these words of mine and does not put them into practice is like a foolish man who built his house on sand. The rain came down, the streams rose, and the winds blew and beat against that house, and it fell with a great crash" (Matthew 7:24-27).

Karen Lodrick came to the place where she said, "I can't stands it no more," and stood against her Identity Thief like a rock. We all have been influenced by the Identity Thief, and Jesus gives us security and assurance against him. In this Sermon on the Mount, Jesus shows us how to have our identity established as "Sons of God" (Matt. 5:9) and live in the blessings of God forever. He concludes this great sermon by challenging us to overcome possible identity theft by establishing our lives on the rock. He is the rock, and when our identity is found in His, we partake of all the authority and power vested in Him, and we can know that we are secure both now and forever.

Those who are seduced by the Identity Thief wash out; their lives are built on the sand. Even though the devil promises his followers more, he is always going to let them wash out because he doesn't care; he desires destruction.

After Jesus had finished telling His followers how they can be the wise men whose lives are built on the rock, the crowds were encouraged and amazed. He taught with such authority. My prayer for all of us is that we will read on and let Him thrill our hearts with a sure understanding of how we have security from identity theft because He is our rock. I have good-news: we can "know it"; we can know that our lives are established on the Rock, and that we have security from identity theft.

Chapter 2
THE JOSEPH STORY

Genesis 37-42

All of my heroes have been preachers, athletes, and leaders. I have a hero in the Old Testament by the name of Joseph; a man who shows me Jesus and myself. Joseph was a son of Jacob, whose name means "deceiver," and for good reason. Joseph would struggle and face the consequences of this pedigree, yet he was able to defer to a higher and nobler identity. We can gain an identity power assist from the life of this Old Testament hero who learned to live out of his true identity in God. For this reason he is my favorite Old Testament character and a true hero of mine. Please allow me to introduce you to my friend.

Joseph was favored by his father. He was given a special multi-colored robe that showed off this favoritism. We might not always feel like we are our Heavenly Father's favorite, but we are. We are the apple of His eye. He tells us we are in His "much more" care and reminds us of how he feeds the birds of the air, and clothes the flowers of the field, and tells us to consider how much more valuable we are to Him than these things that display His glory (Matt 5-6).

John Chapter 1 tells us that God's own son was born a Jew and tried to reach out to His people, but "His own received Him not." Jesus experienced the cold slap in the face we know as rejection, and so did Joseph. Joseph's brothers didn't care for him at all. Perhaps they despised the favoritism that was blatantly obvious. Father Jacob did many special things for Joseph that showed everyone that he was the apple of his eye. Joseph was a big dreamer, and he let his mouth run away from him. He talked matter-of-factly about what God was saying to Him in his dreams. He had outlandish interpretations of these dreams, and he didn't know any better than to share these gems with his brothers. Consequently, they couldn't stand this spoiled big dreamer and even bigger talker who wore the attention-attracting coat.

I remember going to a Nebraska-Colorado football game in Boulder, Colorado. Being a lifelong Big Red fan, my son and I were decked out in red, and our seats were in the middle of black and gold

CU fans. We were given the cold shoulder all game long, and as the Buffs started to win, we were getting antagonized; it was a very uncomfortable feeling.

Let's just say, Joseph tried to go to the game, but he was wearing the wrong letter jacket.

Joseph, in his enthusiasm about his life, explained some of his dreams to his brothers. He told them about shocks of wheat and the sun, moon, and stars. He lacked tact when he told these brothers how the shocks of wheat would be bound into sheaves and they would one day bow to him. And he explained to these brothers that even the sun, the moon, and eleven stars would bow to him. The brothers saw him as a favored little brat with a smart mouth. Joseph hadn't read the book on how to win friends and influence people, so when he explained that his brothers would be bowing to him one day, they were seriously peeved.

The day would come when the brothers were out in the field tending the flock, and they observed Joseph a long way off, so they conspired together a "Kodak Moment." They were going to string up their snot-nosed little brother and let him know how special he really was. They came up with a plan to teach a lesson to this smart aleck little brother once and for all. They would throw him in a cistern, leave him for dead, and then take his special robe back to Dad and deceive this deceiver with Joseph's bloodied robe, telling him he was killed by wild animals.

When my dad was a boy growing up in Grand Island, Nebraska, across the alley from him lived a smart-mouthed little boy. We know him today as the famous talk show host Dick Cavitt. My dad called him little Dickey Cavity and couldn't stand this little runt who had a big pie hole in his head. This little chump would constantly correct my grandpa's grammar and complete his sentences. Both of Dick's parents were English teachers, so even though he was only five or six years old he was a curt, "know it all" brat. With great pleasure, Dad has told me some of the pranks he played on this little grammar corrector, like propping a bucket of water on the basement door and asking Dickey to come down - only to see little Dickey get soaked. Dad told me of another of his ideas: he said he wanted to bind up little Dickey and put him in an old-fashioned, gas powered mangle, a device used to iron things, complete with a wringer used to straighten out creases. Dickey could have used a little straightening out. Dad saw little Dickey as if he were a "Dennis the Menace" and felt this little, smarty-pants "know it all" deserved these come-uppences.

The brothers felt the same way about Joseph; they couldn't stand him, so they bound him and were going to leave him for dead until their older brother persuaded them to sell him to the Ishmaelites who just happened to be passing through at the time. So they sold this seventeen-year-old brat of a brother named Joseph for twenty shekels of silver. Does this type of betrayal sound familiar?

Even though Joseph had been beaten, betrayed, abandoned, and then sold by his brothers, he never forgot who he was in God; he always lived and believed in his true identity. Joseph went to Egypt as a child of God who would serve as a slave. He knew he wore the crown and believed God would raise him up even though his circumstances were depressing. His faith in his true identity would one day be manifest, as Joseph would serve as the prince of Egypt when he wore the crown!

Joseph would exchange possession from the Ishmaelites to the Midianites, and then he would become the possession of Potiphar, who was an official to the Pharoah of Egypt. Even though he was passed around, he never forgot who he was, and by faith he believed God was with him and for him. Joseph was a good-looking, hard-working, and reliable servant in Potiphar's house. Because he lived out of his true identity, he earned more responsibilities, and the blessings of Grace River[3] flowed through Joseph. He was wearing the crown before he wore the crown!

Mrs. Potiphar was a desperate housewife who wanted some attention from Joseph. Perhaps Mr. Potiphar was paying too much attention to other things, like running the Pharaoh's empire. Mrs. Potiphar had too much time on her hands and was watching too many soap operas. She had one playing in her mind, as she was fantasizing

---

[3] *Grace River Living* is the first book written by the author, focusing on the themes of Mount Truth and the Banks of Discipline, which yield the Spirit controlled life. See Appendix #2 on page 220.

about being with this young, good-looking prince of a man named Joseph. She decided to play out this steamy soap opera and made advances toward Joseph.

Like cream that rises to the top of an old-fashioned milk bottle, Joseph was a rising star in Potiphar's house. Success is like a fleeting vapor, and in a moment of indiscretion or false accusation, what we work to attain can be pulled out from under us like a carpet on a slick wood floor. Mrs. Potiphar was about to pull the carpet out from under the crown-wearing young man. For a person to truly be a success, he needs a definition of success that matches his true identity in Jesus—a definition that cannot be blocked. If your definition of success can be intercepted by anyone, it needs to be revamped. Just as we need goals that cannot be blocked, we need a definition of success that can't be blocked by circumstances. Joseph would soon find that his identity in God made him like a rock, strong and secure even though he would be tossed from the heights of the capitol building to the dank cellar of a prison cell.

To me success is "the release of my heart to enable Jesus to be Himself in me, and then He allows me to be myself in Him." If you adopt a definition like this, then you are able to avoid the depression that failure or abandonment can bring. And we can be delivered from the anger that can ferment in our hearts towards those who block us. If we can adopt a good definition of success, soon we will be living as if we are unblockable and rock-like. Another definition I like is, "to wear the CROWN, and help others to wear the CROWN." These definitions are great tools to evaluate how to respond to life's challenges. Our behavior always follows our beliefs, and so we must tell ourselves the truth and let the truth keep us free (John 8:32).

Joseph was ready to face Mrs. Potiphar's lair and false accusations because he was secure in his identity. In Genesis 39:7 we read, "and after a while his master's wife took notice of Joseph and said 'come to bed with me!' But he refused." Joseph tried to reason with this desperate housewife, he thought she would understand that he didn't want to jeopardize his job, and his relationship with Mr. Potiphar. He told her that he valued his trust, and then we see his bright shining identity seeing him through this temptation as he says, "How could I sin against God?" In spite of Joseph's resolve, she kept trying to seduce him, day after day. Mrs. Potiphar, like a hungry dog or a carnal person, desired what she couldn't have more and more.

In her mind she felt that she had to have him; she could have everything else, but her desire was for this young Hebrew. One day after she told Joseph her seductive words, she tried to throw herself on him by grabbing his cloak. She said, "come to bed with me." If Hollywood was writing this script, I am sure it would show Joseph falling into this trap, taking off his shirt, flexing his pecs, showing off his washboard stomach, and satisfying her desires, with Joseph becoming her little pet, a sex slave who would be her "kept" man. But Joseph wasn't drawing his identity from the world, the flesh, or the devil. He lived for an audience of one: Almighty God! Joseph's true identity shined in this steamy moment; his behavior flowed out of his true identity. He fled, and ran from this temptation. And there she was holding his coat (1 Corinthians 10:13)

The Bible says, "The heart of man is deceitful above all things and beyond cure" (Jeremiah 17:9). In just a blink, she devised a wicked scheme. She reasoned she was holding the evidence for the CSI team, and she began to cry as if there had been an attempted rape. She told the servants it was the "Hebrew slave"—notice how she identifies Joseph? She told all who would listen that he tried to abuse her and make sport of her. Like all victim thinkers, she devised a water-tight story that had him tried and convicted. Like all losers, she reasoned if she can't have him, ruin him.

This fabricated account was accepted by Mr. Potiphar, and Joseph was sent to jail with a conviction that could have impacted his identity. But the identity of a rapist just couldn't stick to Joseph. While in jail Joseph's faith and his identity would be severely tested. The name Joseph means "God will add," and "to increase in faithfulness." I am sure there were a lot of quiet moments where Joseph had to pray through and trust His unseen God for the grace to believe the truth about his identity. A lesser man with a shaky identity would most certainly tank in this cell of despair. But I picture Joseph sitting in prison, singing Bob Seger's great song, "Like a Rock," and having the resolve to believe that he was secure in God.

Prison gave Joseph time to reflect on how he was a favored son: his rejection, his position, his false accusation, and his name. I believe that during this time Joseph would cry out to God, and God would comfort him. I am sure Joseph didn't forget God, and God was constantly reassuring him about his plan. Maybe He reminded Joseph about the dreams. Just as Jesus rose from the dead, Joseph was good as dead in the dank prison. But God raises the dead.

The only hope Joseph had was his faith, "Now faith is being sure of what we hope for and certain of what we do not see" (Hebrews 11:1). This definition clearly defines Joseph's situation.

And in Hebrews 11:6 it says, "And without faith it is impossible to please God, because anyone who comes to God must believe that he exists and that He rewards those who earnestly seek Him." I am sure Joseph was earnestly seeking God.

While in this prison, Joseph was growing in faith and pleasing God. He would make friends with a cup-bearer and a baker, and these fellows had been having dreams that aroused their curiosity. They approached Joseph and wanted his help interpreting these dreams. Joseph would not let them flatter him about his gift of interpretations; he reminded them that "interpretations belong to God." He knew who he was and that it was God who brought this word.

Because Joseph was secure in his identity, he didn't hedge on the interpretations of the dreams. The cup-bearer told about a vine with three branches, how they blossomed, and how the clusters ripened into grapes, and how the Pharaoh's cup was filled with wine from these grapes. Joseph explained the dream by saying in three days Pharaoh will lift you up, restore your position, and put his cup in your hand. The only thing Joseph asked was, "remember me." Sure enough, the cup-bearer was restored to his position and the cup was placed again into his hand. But he forgot Joseph.

Jesus said of the communion cup, do this in remembrance of me. Jesus is the Lord God Almighty, and even though He has asked us to remember Him, how often do we forget Him? There are many parallels between the lives of Joseph and Jesus. In this situation, the one who saved the cup-bearer was forgotten; in our lives, the one who saved our souls by giving us His life and the good news is often forgotten. Let's remember the words, "Remember me."

Though Joseph was forgotten by a man, he was not forsaken by God. I believe God and Joseph enjoyed intimate communion in that prison cell, and Joseph kept growing in faith. I am sure Joseph was constantly reminding his human spirit about the dreams God gave him when he was a young boy. I believe it was this word from God that saved Joseph during this time of horrible obscurity in prison.

It is a delight to bring good news, but to share the bad news is a test of our character and our identity. So when the Chief Baker told Joseph about his dream about baskets on his head, Joseph matter-of-factly told him he was going to be hanged, and he was. There are lots of benefits of being secure in one's identity, and not being unstable is one of them.

Two full years would pass after these interpretations were fulfilled, and yet Joseph remained secluded in prison. He had been forgotten by everyone but God. But then the Pharaoh would have some dreams and Joseph would emerge from obscurity and be sought out. Pharaoh had dreamt about cows and corn, fat and skinny cows, and he didn't know what to do with these unnerving dreams.

By Providence, Joseph was remembered, and through God he was able to discern the meaning of the dreams. God let him know there would be seven years of abundant harvests as pictured by the fat cows. And there would be seven years of famine as pictured by the skinny cows. This report was understood by the Pharaoh, and Joseph was elevated and put in charge of implementing a "saving" program. Joseph led this empire to build a grain storage building that would be used to save the people in the region.

Meanwhile, back at the ranch in Jacob's homeland of Israel, the brothers are starving. They hear, "there is grain in Egypt." The brothers' hunger pains drive them to trek to Egypt and request food from the Pharaoh. I am sure by this time that they had forgotten Joseph's dreams, and how he told them they would be like sheaves of wheat and stars bowing before him. But there they were with their hats in their hands, bowing to Joseph and begging for food. God has a way to make a way when there seems to be no way. He is faithful to fulfill His word.

But when the brothers stood before this powerful leader in Egypt, they didn't know this was the younger brother with who they had beaten, abandoned, sold, and deceived their father. And now the tables had turned and they were at Joseph's mercy. Twenty years had passed, and what they saw was a statesman with the ring on his finger, the regal robes, gold chains, the chariot team, and acting with the authority of the throne. Yet, none of these trappings or the prestige of his position had altered Joseph's identity.

Remember, Joseph found his identity in God, but there was a lot of Jacob the deceiver in him too. This story gets even more human as Joseph begins to sift them as wheat. Joseph knows he has them against the wall, and he knows he has a rare opportunity to make some statements and teach some lessons. He vacillates between acting out identities, as a deceiver like his earthly father Jacob, and acting in a magnanimous way, like his Heavenly Father God.

A lot of video tape was running through his mind as he looked at these brothers before him. Paybacks can be really rough, creative, and fun. Or this could be an opportunity to extend the olive branch and show forgiveness. Or he could do both. He was in a position where he could crush these pitiful brothers, teach them a lesson, or turn the other cheek. Joseph really didn't know what to do and so made his brothers jump through some hoops.

So while still hiding his identity, Joseph acted as the governor and accused the brothers of being spies; I am sure this accusation caused them to wet their pants. Joseph interrogated them and found that their father and younger brother Ben were still alive. So he put all but one of the brothers in prison and had the others go for young Ben. I think he wanted to see them sweat.

Good things can happen in men's hearts while they are in prison, and these brothers reflected on how they had mistreated their brother Joseph. They began to express some sincere sorrow and a sense that they were in this predicament because of what they had done. Joseph was listening to these conversations, and I think God was working on his heart; it was filling with the compassion that was consistent with his true identity.

Joseph then released them and had one of the brothers stay back as collateral while the others headed back to Israel with grain in their bags and a special prize on the inside. Just like a Cracker Jack box, when the brothers opened their bags of grain, the silver they had used to make this purchase was inside the bags. Previously they had wet themselves with Joseph's accusation as spies; now I think they soiled themselves as they thought they would be accused of stealing. And knowing men like this, I am sure they had a few choice words to commemorate the situation. They were in a darned if they do, darned if they don't situation. They had to come forward and admit to having this silver.

The time would come for the brothers to return to Egypt because they would run out of grain. So they returned with little Ben, large gifts, and double the silver to make things right with the leaders in Egypt. When Joseph saw the brothers returned and Benjamin with them he had a special dinner for them. Even though Egyptians and Jews were not to ever eat together, Joseph was close. The brothers were scared to have this meal with Joseph, and they still did not know that he was the brother they had betrayed. The brothers were quick to explain the silver situation to the steward; they were assured that everything would be alright. Then they prepared gifts for Joseph. The Proverbs tell us that, "a gift opens the way for the giver and ushers him into the presence of the great" (18:16), and now the brothers were about to witness the great Joseph.

When he saw his brother Benjamin, his brother from the same mother, Joseph was deeply moved and he excused himself to go and weep. Then he washed his face to restore looking fresh. Just when Joseph was about to reveal his true identity, he had yet another prank up his sleeve. He had the steward fill the brothers' sacks with as much food as could be stuffed in them, and then Joseph's own silver cup was placed in Benjamin's sack. After the brothers were on their way, Joseph sent a posse after them, had them arrested, and brought back for a trial. They were arrested for stealing the Governor's silver cup and, worse yet, their little brother was going to be in big trouble. I am sure these brothers were about ready to slit their wrists, and for sure they feared that they would be put to death.

Young Benjamin was to be made into an Egyptian slave because the silver cup was found in his sack; the brothers were to return home to Jacob, without Ben. Judah saw that the brothers were up a creek and offered himself as a substitute, a trade for Ben; he offered to become a slave because I am sure he feared his father couldn't handle such a loss. Then Joseph could no longer control his emotions; he cried out and ordered every one of his servants to leave his presence then he revealed himself to his brothers. He wept so loudly that the Pharaoh's people heard him. Joseph said to his brothers, "I am Joseph! Is my father still living?" But his brothers were not able to answer this, because they were terrified at his presence. Then Joseph said to his brothers, "Come close to me." When they had done so, he said, "I am your brother Joseph, the one you sold into Egypt." His true identity had been revealed, and his faith in God enabled the love to flow so that he could save them. He reminded them that God had providentially made this great provision. The love and forgiveness was flowing as Joseph was able to express how what was done to him was forgiven. God had made it clear to Joseph that he was to respond to the evil that had been done to him by returning good instead (Romans 12).

There is a great identity verse in Romans 8:28-29 which says, "And we know that in all things God works for the good of those who love Him, who have been called according to His purpose. For those God foreknew he also predestined to be conformed to the likeness of His Son, that He might be the firstborn, among many brothers." This passage tells the story of Joseph and his brothers, as favoritism, rejection, abandonment, betrayal, false accusation, obscurity, and a thin line of faith was used by God to provide miraculously for his people, and in the process he was making a Christ-like man out of Joseph.

At first Joseph was too proud to be seen crying, but his identity and his love shone through in this very touching scene. Just as God can not deny His true identity, neither can we when we desire to follow God's will. Joseph knew he couldn't continue playing this charade, now he wanted to release Grace River to his brothers.

Joseph affirmed to his brothers that God had called him into this position to save them. He then went about providing a new home for his family so they could survive the famine. Think of it: because

Joseph chose to live out his true identity, his family was able to have the "fat of the land"—because of grace. Best of all, Egypt was theirs because they belonged to God, and God was releasing His grace through Joseph.

Father Jacob was revived by this good news, and Joseph was able to reconnect with his earthly father. This must have been glorious. I wish Hollywood would make such a movie. This story has such a happy ending because truth set these brothers free—the truth of Joseph's identity in God!

Identity became so important to Joseph that he chose special names for his sons. He named one Manasseh, which means "God has made me forget my troubles." And he named the other Ephraim because God had made him fruitful. These great Grace River names would serve to remind Joseph of who he was in God and what God wants to do through us.

Joseph could have reverted to a fleshly life, chosen to live like a "chip off the old block," and lived out his days as a deceiver like his daddy Jacob, the manipulator and victim. Instead he chose to draw his true identity from his Heavenly Father. Our behaviors always follow our beliefs; there were times in Joseph's life that he acted more like Jacob, but the Holy Spirit was able to refine his heart in such a way that he would always be remembered as a Christ-like, forgiving figure in the Old Testament. We have the same choice: what identity are we going to live out of? Our earthly father's? Or our Heavenly Father's?

Joseph is a great example of a man who chose to live out of his true identity in God. This faith choice made him like a rock with solid character. We, too, can be heroes to our brothers by choosing to live out of our true identity and really "Know it!"

Chapter 3
DILUTED MAN

James 1:12-22, Proverbs 6:24-29, Matthew 5:28

The first time I saw Stu he wasn't paying his wife the attention she deserved. Stu was trying to be the life of the party and was seeking attention from everyone, even other women, at the cook-out on our patio. I observed the hurt on Kathy's face, but Stu was oblivious to her and her needs. He wasn't even paying attention to their precious little girls that were toddling along. Stu was an identity crisis happening right before my eyes. He acted like a rock-like stud, yet he was being stupid. He would quickly identify with Jesus Christ, yet he integrated nothing of Jesus into his relationships. His life was about to wash out and he didn't even "know-it."

I know it is hard to imagine a twenty-six year old, attention grabbing, insensitive, super competitive and porn-addicted man as a good man, but Stu really is a good man who had become a *diluted* man. He had been building his life on loose gravel; there was nothing consistent or solid about him. He would tell you that he wanted his life, his marriage, and his family to be established on the rock, but he never sought out the discipleship or mentoring to shore up his life. This story, even though it is true and the names have been changed, shows what God can do to a diluted man. God loves to take the diluted and add the concrete of Godly character, and the rebar (steel) of Godly counsel to establish people on the rock Christ Jesus.

There really are no excuses for Stu to hide behind. Today he is well aware of his wrongs and has chosen to take responsibility for his life, his mistakes, and his moral failures. James, the earthly brother of the Lord Jesus, was familiar with trials and had this to say about hardship, "Consider it pure joy, my brothers, whenever you face trials of many kinds, because you know that the testing of your faith develops perseverance. Perseverance must finish its work so that you may be mature and complete not lacking anything" (James 1:2-3). This classic scripture has been proven in Stu's life. He has gone through many trials, and he is coming through them by faith and has become a man who wears the crown of pure gold that reflects his new character.

Stu is the oldest of eight children. His parents had all boys except for the second youngest, a little girl. These busy parents spaced their children one year apart and thus made themselves busier. There were lots of mouths to feed, diapers to change, and shoes to tie. And even though these parents had a sincere Christian faith, they acted out of the religious attitude they were raised with.

These hard working parents naturally raised up hard working children who would learn to compete. These children had to compete at the dinner table and try to elbow the other children out so they could get enough to eat. If you have ever seen a momma robin feeding her nest full of chicks you get the picture. The boys became top-notch high school wrestlers, soccer players, hockey players, and all of them sport great bodies with strong arms with well defined pecs and biceps. They are some of the hardest workers I have ever seen.

Stu is so athletic he can do a standing back flip like it is nothing, and at only five feet nine inches tall he is an excellent basketball player. The three brothers that I know are all good looking guys, athletic, good natured, and moral. They love to laugh, and give each other a ribbing, but for the most part they are respect based guys who love God and sincerely care for people. I have seen these guys stop their own work and all pitch in to move a single mother who needed their help into a new apartment. Or stop and help a stranger on the side of the road that had a flat tire. These are great guys, guys that make you think there is hope for the world, and guys you would like living next door.

Even though these guys are top notch they can overwhelm you with their energy, passion, curiosity and intensity. I enjoy their competitiveness, and like engaging them in deep and stimulating conversation even in arguments. It doesn't take long to see that Stu and his brothers are super-charged, red-blooded, testosterone filled and fully alive guys. They do outdoor landscape and tree removal work and they can clear and clean an acre of shrubs in no time or landscape a new lot with ease. But, when it comes to having intimacy with women, Stu is all thumbs. Don't get me wrong, he is outgoing and charming, but not the most understanding.

He looks back to his relationship with his mother, and believes that she was harsh and critical of him. Because he was the oldest son perhaps she expected him to grow up fast and help out more than he did. I think she was just extremely busy and had lots on her plate. Certainly with all these mouths to feed there were lots of messy dishes piling up next to the kitchen sink. She probably didn't intend to ignore his needs, but she didn't have the time to find out Stu's love language[4] (words of affirmation, gifts, touch, quality time or acts of service) and learn how to communicate to him in that special way. She needed him to help her with her large squad, and even though Stu loves to help out today, perhaps back then he felt like a misfit to his mom and consequently he didn't receive the affection he longed for. He doesn't remember hearing the affirming words "I love you," or "I'm proud of you," and being embraced with the physical touch that means so much.

While the boys were growing up quickly, at the age of twelve Stu remembers a neighbor boy who brought a Playboy Magazine® into their hide out. Stu remembers to this day the shock and awe of these pictures as these images exploded into his mind. He wasn't immediately hooked on this type of pornography, but he did like the sense of discovery, the adventure, and the adrenaline rush of seeing these women exposed in air-brushed pictures.

Stu's mom and dad kept boundaries as best they could with their houseful of children. But their rules-based religion of "dos and don'ts" didn't impart to Stu the strong sense of identity he needed to combat the evil that had come into his hideout. Even though he remembers trusting in Jesus at a young age, he doesn't remember being taught how to live out of His righteous identity in Jesus. Consequently, Stu didn't know how to "wear the Crown!" (Isaiah 61:3), and put on Christ, and be clothed in righteousness, or how to establish biblical order in his life, so he could live as a worshipper and walk in nobility.[5] Stu would learn more about his true identity during

---

[4] Dr. Gary D. Chapman, *The Five Love Languages*, Northfield Publishing, Chicago, IL, 1995.
[5] Sid explains the C.R.O.W.N. in his book, *Grace River Living*, Chapter 24.

his time of trial that had now knocked on his door when that dirty magazine came in with the neighbor boy.

James says, "Blessed is the man who perseveres under trial, because when he has stood the test, he will receive the crown of life that God has promised to those who love Him" (James 1:12).

Stu was going to learn about wearing the crown the hard way, through trials. He didn't know that his behavior flows out of the way he sees himself, or as I like to say it, out of his identity. He simply saw himself as a red-blooded, inquisitive young man who was revved up by looking at these Playboy® pictures. And at twelve years of age he didn't become an instant porn addict, but the Identity Thief was leaning against this door. By the time Stu turned eighteen the door was knocked completely open and porn's potency was in effect. Porn was now the "go-to" thing for Stu. When he needed a little pick me up, he gazed at porn. He didn't know that he was attempting to meet his need for affirmation and affection with porn. But this is what sin is. Sin is going to something other than God to get a buzz or try to fix ourselves.

The Identity Thief has a way of taking our natural affections and turning them into sin. The Apostle Paul said, "no temptation has seized you except what is common to man. And God is faithful; He will not let you be tempted beyond what you can bear. But when you are tempted, He will also provide you with a way out so that you can stand up under it" (I Cor. 10:13). Because Stu didn't understand the Identity Thief's ways, and God's way out through applying the principles of our true identity in Jesus, Stu was stuck in a sin box. The irony is that his flesh loved this behavior, he was tantalized by these pictures. He learned how to masturbate, so he went deeper into sin and was hooked on his sin habit. He really didn't want out of this sin box because in these sensual moments, he felt big, strong and manly. And in his imagination he pictured women being impressed with him and desiring him.

Being stuck in this box, Stu didn't think there was anyone he could talk to about these behaviors. Sure his conscience was uncomfortable, but maybe he could keep this private. James tells us how to address these problems by saying, "When tempted, no one should say, God is tempting me." For God cannot be tempted by evil, nor does he tempt anyone; but each one is tempted when, by his own evil desires, he is dragged away and enticed" (James 1:12-14).

Stu could easily blame his failures on his parents, his environment, his religious upbringing, and his church community. He could say, "My mom and dad didn't prepare me for puberty, they didn't help me learn how to battle temptation with spiritual warfare and understanding my identity in Jesus." He could even blame the print media, MTV, and the movies for the ways they teased him and tempted him with sexual images. But it doesn't do him any good to blame, and it especially doesn't do him any good to blame God. He knew God well enough to know that God doesn't have any element of sin in Him. God could not mislead or tempt him. Stu hasn't blamed God, and he knows that he must take responsibility for his life.

James makes it clear our relationship with God and our identity in Him helps us win the battle of believing the truth. We must take responsibility for our beliefs and soon the proper actions will follow. The Word of God is clear, "Each one is tempted when by his own evil desires he is dragged away and enticed" (James 1:15). Stu, by sinning like he did, ultimately got the crap kicked out of him in spiritual, emotional, mental and relational ways.

Stu is learning to take responsibility for his actions, but like when he straps on his snowboard and starts traversing an icy Colorado ski slope, he hit a crusty ice patch. Stu's life began to slip off the mountain and spin out of control. He went from turning pages in dirty magazines to channel surfing, looking for more and more stimulating images.

While in his early twenties Stu met a beautiful young blond named Kathy. He fell in lust with her and quickly got married. He failed to find out if she was a healthy young lady emotionally, mentally, relationally, physically and spiritually. He failed to ask the important questions about health and compatibility, and consequentially he found himself in a very unhealthy relationship, both because of his unhealthy thoughts and hers. And he failed to really address the glitches in his upbringing, his poor self concept, and his mental health because of his porn use. If you are a young person contemplating marriage, please take the time to think about health on all fronts. Stu just followed his nose into marriage and hoped things would work out, when in fact there were serious red flags all around this relationship.

There are always lots of "shouldas, couldas, wouldas" when it comes to our actions, but if Stu would have taken the time to study and find that his love language (the way he best gives and receives love). was both "words of affirmation" and healthy and affirming "physical touch", he would have been forced to face the truth about Kathy's view of sexuality. During her child hood years she was sexually abused and had become repulsed by men and the thoughts of sex. Here he was thinking that marriage would satisfy his sexual appetites, but his wife's issues complicated his marriage bed would give the Identity Thief more ways to attempt to destroy their lives. They both were completely unsatisfied with their marriage.

One of the sad ironies of this story is that Stu was a youth Pastor and was passionate and gifted in helping young people. One day he went to his church office to check his e-mail and found a very sensual and inviting picture on his monitor. This was his introduction to internet porn, a venue that was more interactive and more attractive. He began to feast on these sites and got lost gazing at these luscious beauties. Like a dog that picks up a scent and then can no longer respond to its master, Stu was on a trail that was leading to his destruction; he was now addicted to porn. It was insidious how the more he fixed his gaze upon these pictures, the more his appetite for sex increased; it became insatiable.

The Identity Thief had turned a good guy into a porn addicted wreck waiting to happen. Like an alcoholic or a crack addict, Stu was now driven to getting his porn "fix." This constant urge was now controlling his life. And Stu's good heart and good sense was now kaput. As stimulated as Stu was by the access to internet porn, the Identity Thief was about to spring some new spice into Stu's lap: the strip clubs.

By attending strip clubs Stu thought he was getting even more of his "needs" met. He loved how these beautiful girls would smile and dance for him. He wished his wife would try to engage him sexually, but in the experience of the club he felt the affirmation he longed for. The women made him feel sexy and desirable. He would quickly forget about the money he was paying for these nods of approval and admiration.

Even though the strip clubs gave a false sense of intimacy, these women were playful and Stu loved the attention. This form of porn completely captured his ego and his mind, and by now his conscience was completely numb. From an identity standpoint he didn't care for his life or reputation anymore and was trying to forget about Jesus. And little did he know that these experiences were causing him to devalue and disrespect Kathy. The comparison of Kathy to these beauties also complicated Stu's relationship at home by making him even more insensitive and disappointed

Stu had bought the lies the Identity Thief had been telling him. "This is your private world, what you do here is your own business, you are a big boy and you can do what you want, you are not hurting any one." The Identity Thief always steals from those he makes his friends and he was about to pull off a heist.

James says, "Then after desire has conceived, it gives birth to sin, and sin, when it is full-grown, gives birth to death" (James 1:15).

God's Word is true and is always proved true, so Stu was about to experience death in the biblical sense of the word: it means separation. His sex addiction was now full blown and the seeds of porn in his life were now full grown. These seeds had in them the DNA of destruction and alienation.

Stu's house crumbled in what looks like a few fleeting moments, yet the termites of porn had been eating at its foundation and rafters for a long time. His wood was rotten and all it took for his house to fall was a little breeze and a misstep.

Kathy had become so disappointed in Stu that she accused him of touching their daughter inappropriately. She took her cell phone and threatened to push 911 and summon the police to their home. In the next few minutes the negative impact the Identity Thief had been working in Stu's life came to fruition. He was so insecure in his identity that he panicked and tried to wrestle the phone from Kathy. She eventually made the call; the power of sin in Stu was going to come down hard with some severe consequences.

When Kathy pushed the buttons on the cell phone she was also pushing Stu's buttons and the ensuing wrestling match for the phone turned the charges against Stu into domestic violence; he was hand cuffed and sent to jail. Later he would be charged with a third degree assault and have to spend hundreds of hours trying to sort out his life, renew his mind, save his marriage and only hope to see his precious little girls again.

By the grace of God Stu was able to come to his senses and give the Identity Thief a strong stiff arm and begin to resist him (James 4:7). He began to seek out godly men for counsel and began attending all the required classes for being accused as a sex offender. Who would have thought that those glances at a Playboy® magazine would culminate in jail, an ankle bracelet, a divorce, only being able to see his girls with supervised visits for short periods of time, and session after session of counseling. And most of this counseling was abusive towards Stu. No one would believe his story. They all said he was in denial about not being an abusive person. He received bad marks from the agencies though all he had to do to get high marks was to lie and speak an untruth about wrongful touching.

The Identity Thief has tried to take this man of God, imperfect as he is, and rename him a, felon, a sex addict, a perpetrator, an abuser, a molester, a convict, a dead-beat dad, and a menace to society. All of these labels hurt Stu, but he had to be humbled by the consequences of his sins before he would take his situation seriously. The truth of his true identity in Jesus is now setting him free to grow and eventually he will become the dad God wants him to be. A lesser man would have run away and given up on his responsibilities, and said the heck with it all. But, by the grace of God, Stu has stood in there, paid the price, and he is seeing his life and true identity redeemed.

Talk about price! The costs are astronomical, the ankle bracelet and monitor that he has to carry (he can not be more than fifty feet from the back pack that carries this transmitter so his whereabouts are always documented). costs him two hundred and thirty dollars a month. The counseling sessions are about fifty dollars a session, and to pay the lawyers for both his defense and even for his ex-wife is outrageous. The time away from his work to try to work through the court cases has cost him in very expensive ways with high costs of equipment rental for his landscape business and new work. Just from a financial standpoint he is paying more than two thousand dollars a month, to do the right things regarding reconciliation and recovery.

And the price has only increased, as Stu did something that has caused the price to escalate. He found out Kathy's and the girls new address through a church member. He picked up some McDonald's "Happy Meals" ® and dropped them off on their doorstep. As he was driving away he called to tell them that Daddy left a surprise on their doorstep. I believe his actions were innocent, but Kathy's lawyer and the victim's advocate have convinced the Judge that this act has caused Kathy to live in fear of Stu showing up at their door, which is a violation of the restraining order. The last time Stu checked in with the probation officer he was thrown in prison for this act. Stu now calls himself stupid for this breach, and this negative self-talk is something the Identity Thief entices.

James offers some very practical counsel here as he says:

"Don't be deceived, my dear brothers. Every good and perfect gift is from above, coming down from the Father of the heavenly lights, who does not change like shifting shadows. He chose to give us birth through the Word of truth that we might be a kind of first fruits of all He created.
My dear brothers, take note of this: Everyone should be quick to listen, slow to speak and slow to become angry, for man's anger does not bring about the righteous life that God desires. Therefore, get rid of all moral filth and the evil that is so prevalent and humbly accept the Word planted in you, which can save you.
Do not merely listen to the Word, and so deceive yourselves, do what it says" (James 1:16-22).

Stu has leaned into his pain and embraced his trial as the hammer and chisel God is using to make him like Jesus. He knows that God is using this trial help him overcome the Identity Thief and make him into a more perfect and solid man (A work in process). He is becoming a man with a tender heart toward God and others. He has a new found ability to listen to others, feel their pain and be sincerely sensitive. He is learning about love. He weeps for his ex-wife and their little girls. He knows that even though his porn addiction doesn't mean he was a child abuser or a sex offender, he is learning to humble his heart and show contrition.

During his last court appearance he had to face the music about his insensitivity to his former wife. He heard her say under oath that he used the Bible to get her to submit to him by quoting, "wives submit to your husbands as to the Lord" (Ephesians 5:22) and tried to manipulate her with guilt and shame to do what he wanted. He had to be grieved to his core when he heard this testimony because these actions showed how he didn't understand that he was to lay his life down for his wife and make sacrifices for her. If he had been acting out of an identity in Jesus he wouldn't have been insensitive or demanding in the name of religion. With a religious spirit, he would have been washing her feet, listening, and regarding her as more important than himself (Phil 2:1-5).

Having heard this testimony I couldn't help but think about the Pastor of a church in McMinnville, Tennessee who did some of the same things to his wife. She got so tired of living the double life, acting so "Christian" at church and coming home to this kind of abuse from him, that she shot and killed him. You would think that Mary Winkler would be serving a long prison sentence, but the court so sympathized with the abuse she lived with from her guilt-laying preacher husband so much so that she was only given a 210 day prison sentence, and required to get some counseling to deal with post traumatic stress. When a man uses religion and other controlling methods to get the behaviors he wants out of his wife he is to be despised and pitied. Obviously Mary Winkler's husband Matthew was living a lie. It is a grievous thing to see so much hypocrisy, and sad to realize that Mary felt that she had no way to get help. She might not have even known what true spirituality really looked like. I cry when I think about how there are so many people who have no clue as to what love really is, because they are only living what they have known.

They live the identity they believe they are, and this preacher didn't know how to live Jesus at home (*Newsweek* Aug. 17th, 2007).

At present Stu is being delivered from his "go-to" habit of viewing porn. His flesh still craves this rush, but he is learning to defer to the Holy Spirit and rely on God's strength (Phil. 4:13). He is learning to idle down his motor and pay attention to authorities, and to listen to those God has put in his life. He nor longer allows himself to defend or explain away wrong actions. He has exchanged his short fuse for a long extension cord that reaches into the heart of God. He is appropriating the patience of God in every area of his life. He now knows that when he feels anger welling up inside of his heart to diffuse these emotions by realizing who he is in Jesus, and remembering that no one can block his real goal of being like Jesus (Anger is often caused by blocked goals, Stu is becoming unblock able by the Identity Thief because he now has better and unblockable goals)

Stu has been studying the Fruit of the Spirit in Galatians 5:22-23[6] and is starting to understand how to get to patience and self-control. Paul said, "but the fruit of the Spirit is love, joy, peace, patience, kindness, goodness, faithfulness, gentleness and self-control. Against such things there is no law." He is learning to live in the love of God and know that he is secure in His identity. Knowing this wonderful love gives him great joy, and makes him strong. The combination of love's-security and joy's-strength makes him to be a peace and keeps him stable. This reality enables him to live contented in God and find true patience. The result of love, joy peace, and patience is making Stu sincerely kind, which is the natural way he responds to people now. Therefore, he has a transformed character and has become a good man, enabling him to be a faithful man who is gentle because he is walking in humility. The result of these steps in the fruit of the Spirit is resulting in self-control which is giving Stu victory over porn and every other sin. This is what is making him a beautiful man (See Pyramid of Victory in the Appendix at the back of this book)

---

[6] See Appendix #1, Pyramid to Victory, on page 219.

It is no problem now for Stu to see why it is so important for him to get rid of all moral filth and reject many of our culture's forms of entertainment because it arouses his sensual sin-craving flesh. In Stu's younger days he would act like he heard the Word of God and pretend that he was obeying, but now he is sincere about being a doer of the Word. For a couple of years now I have been privileged to meet with Stu and help him grow in his identity in Jesus. It has been my pure joy!

He knows that unless he disciplines his thoughts his behaviors can wash out the new foundation he is building with the Lord. He is becoming a beautiful man because the trails he has gone through are making him like Jesus, and the Spirit of God is helping him reach the victory of self-control.

It would be easy for Stu to play at life like he is a victim, but he is choosing responsibility instead. He has had to serve a couple of jail stints for the wrongs he has done, and each time he has gone in and served the other inmates as a servant. He has helped to lead some of the Prison Chapel services by playing worship songs on a keyboard. Stu has had to face the music about his broken relationships and he cries when he realizes that he may not be able to watch his little girls grow up. But he has come to the blessed place where he knows that he can "Know-it". He now knows that Jesus is his life and he is to follow in his footsteps. I can tell you with confidence that he was once diluted, but Stu in now firmly established on the Rock Christ Jesus. He was once stupid, but now this "crown wearing" Stu is growing in wisdom. Now living by relying on Mt. Truth, he is developing his Banks of Discipline and today he is flowing in the Spirit in Grace River.

Chapter 4
BE A MENORAH

Our identity as bright shining lights.
Matthew 5:14-16, John 8-10

The Bible has a classic start to it, "In the beginning God created the heavens and the earth. Now the earth was formless and empty, darkness was over the face of the deep, and the Spirit of God was hovering over the waters. And God said, 'Let there be light' and there was light" (Genesis 1:1-3).

I am claustrophobic, so it took a lot of arm twisting to get me to go into the Cave of the Winds in Colorado Springs. As much as I am fascinated by stalactites and stalagmites, I would never be a spelunker and spend time exploring in caves; besides, those bats give me the creeps. While down in the cave, we came to a place where the guide asked us to cover our watches and cell phones and the flashlights were turned off. Total darkness is stunning!

Ever since Edison discovered the right filament, people have had light 24/7, but in the beginning there was darkness. The Bible points out the dramatic contrast between darkness and light throughout the Bible. It is more than a great bit of trivia to note that the Bible begins with darkness and ends with a very glorious and unusual light, provided by a glorious light source. For a moment now, just close your eyes and imagine your life without light. You can't, because you have seen light.

Jesus, who called himself the "light of the world," said, "Whoever follows me will never walk in darkness, but will have the light of life" (John 8:12). During the winter festival of Hanukkah Jesus was in Jerusalem and John makes an interesting mention about Jesus' itinerary. The Bible says, "then came the Feast of Dedication at Jerusalem. It was winter, and Jesus was in the temple area walking in Solomon's Colonnade" (John 10:22). From this text it is safe to assume that Jesus was there to celebrate the Festival of Lights, also known as the Jewish Holy Festival of Hanukkah.

When I was a ten year old boy, I invited my good friend Matt Greenberger to my home to play with my Hot Wheels® set. I remember asking Matt what he was hoping to get as a gift for Christmas. To my astonishment, Matt told me that his family didn't celebrate Christmas; I remember feeling so sorry for him. Later my mother explained to me that Matt's family was Jewish and that they celebrated eight nights of Hanukkah where each night the members of the family opened a little gift. After I learned of these eight nights of opening gifts I didn't feel so sorry for him. What I didn't know was the beautiful Hebrew story behind this Festival of Lights. The Jews celebrate Hanukkah close to the same time Christians celebrate the birth of Jesus, known as Christmas.

The Jewishness of the Gospel makes it shine brighter; this story makes us see how Jesus lights up our "temples", and how we can be a menorah, a beautiful nine candle holder in the shape of a tree. The more we become like Jesus, the more Jewish we will look and act. This story about the menorah will encourage all of us to add this great symbol to our holiday celebration. The attendance of Jesus at this festival tells us many things about Jesus. He loved to remember the "His-story", and he enjoyed the celebration. Certainly Jesus was the light and the life of the parties he attended! (Pun intended). Once you reflect upon this story you will see the irony of Jesus calling himself the "light of the world", or in this case the "menorah of the world."

Two hundred years before Jesus came to earth in a physical form, the Jews were living unto themselves in the land of Israel, even though it was controlled by the Seleucid King of Syria. Therefore the Jews paid taxes to Syria and were under its authority, but they were free to work and practice their faith. About twenty five years later, Antiochus IV Epihanes was on the throne. In his disdain for the Jews he forced them to do things that went against their beliefs. He forced the Greek culture on the Jews and forbid the study of the Torah, the first five books of the Old Testament. As an intentional offense, he built an altar to the Greek god Zeus in the temple in 167.

The story of Hanukkah involves Mattathias, a Jewish priest, and his five sons John, Simon, Eleazer, Jonathon, and Judah who led a rebellion against Antiochus. Judah became known as Judah Maccabee

(Judah the "Hammer"). By 166 BCE Mattathias had died, and Judah took his place as leader in the struggle. According to the Talmud, oil was needed for the lamp in the Temple, which was supposed to burn throughout the day and night. In the midst of the struggle, there was only enough oil to burn for one day, yet miraculously, it burned for eight. By 165 BCE the Jewish revolt against the Seleucid monarchy was successful. The temple was liberated and rededicated. After recovering Jerusalem and the temple, Judah ordered the temple to be cleansed, a new altar to be built in the place of the polluted one, and new holy vessels to be made. The Festival of Hanukkah was instituted to celebrate the miracle of the oil.

As with so many God stories, there are stories within the story! In this story we see that once again God's children were in bondage and forced to live in an oppressed situation. Yet, just like with Moses, and Joseph, God raises up a deliverer and Mattathias the priest along with his sons bring a gutsy restoration. We need to see Jesus as our deliverer and our restorer, and because He is the light of the world, he is able to lead us in conquest of many dark places. After this initial battle is won, the first thing on the agenda is to restore the temple and dedicate it unto worshipping God.

When a person becomes a Christian they need to learn who they are in Jesus and know that they are now a temple (identity) of the living God (1 Cor. 3:16). Then we need to learn about the importance of being constantly dedicated to God, and make ourselves a living sacrifice to God on a daily basis (Romans 12:1-2). So just as the Temple area was a place where God's Children experienced God in a special way, so now in our hearts we know God is in us. Just as Judah ordered the temple to be cleansed, we experience a cleansing in our own hearts and lives as the Holy Spirit begins to "clean-house." There are sins we repent from (turn away), and new Godly disciplines to establish, so we can enjoy life in His Grace River.

It was said of Jesus, "zeal for your house will consume me" (John 2:17). The same could be said for Mattathias as He rallied his sons and God's children to take back that which belonged to God. The same is true of us, as Jesus invades our lives and restores His order in our lives; he kicks out the idols, and cleans up the rubbish. And before long we are living out of our true identity and can hardly remember our lives when it was under foreign occupation. But, we need to remember that Satan is an Identity Thief, and will try to bring bondage back to our lives. The key to remaining free is to say thank you to Jesus and worship Him. When we do this our light shines bright and the devil can't stand being around the light, he loves darkness. So say thank you to God and be a menorah! Let your light shine, for the Devil loves darkness and hates the light. For that matter, sing praises to God! The Devil hates praise, but God inhabits his praises.

Imagine what Jesus was thinking year after year as he attended this Festival of Lights, and reflected on Mattathias's zeal, the commitment of these sons and the nation, and how the temple was restored. But, when He thought of the lamp light shining in the temple area, I think He understood the price that would be paid, and the pain and suffering it would cost him so we could be a menorah. The lamp in the temple was in a beautiful golden lamp stand that required clear and pure olive oil to burn the way God wanted it to.

Every Jew who had studied the Torah knew the Divine orders God had established for His Temple. In Exodus 27:20 God said to the priests "command the Israelites to bring you clear oil of pressed olives for the light so that the lamp may be kept burning. In the tent of Meeting, outside the curtain that is in front of the Testimony. Aaron and his sons are to keep the lamp burning before the Lord from evening till morning. This is to be an everlasting ordinance among the Israelites for generations to come."

In this law God gives some very detailed instructions as to how things were to be set up so His people could worship Him in a holy way. Everything He writes has spiritual and practical significance. Some people think the study of these laws is boring, but it can captivate our hearts when we compare these mandates to the New Testament letter to the Hebrews and see how Jesus was our perfect High Priest.

Not just any oil will do for the lamp in God's Temple area. This had to be the sacred, pure and clear oil. His clear olive oil was from pressed unripened olives that were crushed and mashed. Then this pulpy mash was put in a basket with a cloth lining and under pressure of heavy weights the oil would seep through it and would drip to the bottom. Slowly the clear pure oil would fill the container at the bottom of the olive press.

I believe every year Jesus reflected on this great story and would ponder Gethsemane which is also called the Mount of Olives. Gethsemane means "the olive press", and in both a physical and spiritual way Jesus experienced the pressure of Himself being in the "olive press." Just as olives were crushed, and turned into pulp and then squeezed, Jesus himself was put under extreme pressure and his purity of His identity and motives became obvious to all. He went to this everyday place to pray with His disciples, they could hardly stay awake, but Jesus allowed the weight of His purpose, and the reality of the cross to press in on Him.

This crushing and purifying process shows us both the humanity and the pure holiness of His Godly character. There was no sin in Jesus that had to be separated out, but He did have to experience the painful anguish in His soul so we could come to Him as our perfect High priest knowing full well that He understood our pain. On this same evening He was betrayed by Judas, and all of us know how painful it is when friends turn away from us in our hard times. And Peter had boastfully announced that he would stand with Him, go to prison for Him and even die for Him. Yet Jesus had to tell Peter he was more thunder than rain and that he would deny him three times before the rooster would crow in the morning.

During this very intense time of prayer we see what is most important to Jesus, he knows that he will be arrested and crucified on a cross the next day. Jesus prays for the disciples and He gives them back to the Father acknowledging that they belong to Him. He prays for them to believe, for I think he knows that these traumatic events are going to shake them up. He prays for God to keep them in the world, even though they will be hated because of the Word Jesus taught them. He wants them to know that they are not of the world, but to be a good influence to the world. He wants them to know that they are loved and their identity is secure in His love. He prays, "Holy Father, protect them by the power of your name—the name you gave me—so that they may be one as we are one" (John 17: 11). And He asks that they would be sanctified in the truth and then He affirms that the Word is the truth. And he prays for the world to believe, to encourage this He prays time and time again for unity. He asks that "these and those", that both the Jews and the Gentiles, would experience oneness together in the Father. He concludes this agonizing and wholehearted prayer by letting the Father know that He wants his disciples to be with Him again and to see His glory. And he reaffirms their identity of them being in Him, and of Him (Jesus) being in them (I get the feeling of birth pangs during this powerful prayer time).

Dr. Luke, the writer of the Gospel of Luke, and one of these disciples reported that the pressure of this prayer time was so intense that Jesus even prayed, "Father, if you are willing, take this cup from me; yet not my will but your be done" (Luke 22:42). This prayer in the garden of Gethsemane was really a pressing prayer. What a back drop, as I can see olive oil draining out of the press and baskets of olives waiting to be crushed.

Luke gives us a rare medical insight into the excruciating pressure Jesus was under as he was praying for His disciples down through the ages, and the pressing reality of the torture He would endure this next day, as He would soon be arrested, and go through the mockery of an unjust trial, be turned over to the crowds, mocked, beaten, scourged and forced to carry a cross up the hill called Golgolatha. This would require great physical exertion, yet emotionally He was being ravaged by the betrayal, and the fact that His disciples fell asleep during this prayer time, He was upset that they couldn't even pray for this hour. This most important and agonizing hour on the Mt. of Olives where he was being drained of His emotional strength, His disciples couldn't stay awake and pray with Him.

Luke says, "An angel from heaven appeared to Him and strengthened Him. And being in anguish He prayed more earnestly and His sweat became like drops of blood falling to the ground" (Luke 22:44). Medical doctors have defined this co-mingling of sweat and blood seeping from the pores, as Hematidrosis. This condition is caused by extreme anguish, strain and sensitivity. And now not a one of us can come to Jesus and say, "Jesus you don't understand my stress!"

By three o'clock in the afternoon, Jesus had already been nailed to the cross and hanging suspended for six hours when the sky became dark. Jesus while hanging on this cross had the grace to pronounce forgiveness on all who where there as He uttered, "Father forgive them for they don't know what they are doing." And then in the darkness He committed His spirit to the Father and then He breathed His last breath. In this sacrificial death I see Jesus as the Lamb of God as the once for all time sacrifice, whose blood was now able to forgive all who would believe.

I also see Jesus as the light of the world, who like in the days of Antiochus Ephanies had the temple desecrated only to have Mattathias lead a revolt and see to it that the temple was restored while the lamp was lit (and miraculously stayed lit) with one day's worth of oil that would keep burning for eight days, until the fresh pressed clear oil would be ready. Jesus the light of the world, the menorah of the world had died, the light was out and the world was dark. All hopes seemed dashed and the people were in despair. The disciples were filled with doubts, and were depressed. But, up from the grave He arose, the Holy Spirit raised Him, He was resurrected and like fresh oil in the lamp, the light in Jesus was bright.

Isaiah a Jewish prophet from long ago predicted, "Nevertheless, there will be no more gloom for those who were in distress. In the past he humbled the land of Zebulon and the land of Naphtali, but in the future he will honor Galilee of the Gentiles, by the way of the sea, along the Jordan—The people walking in darkness, have seen a great light; on those living in the land of the shadow of death a light has dawned" (Isaiah 9:2).

Often this passage is often referred to a as a Christmas text that predicts the birth of the birth of the Messiah, but the resurrection of Jesus by the Holy Spirit brings light to the world in a way that it will never go out. He is the everlasting lamp, who can now fill the "temples", the physical bodies, the "jars of clay", with the treasure. His presence can now consume every person who believes. Therefore because Jesus was raised from the dead, we can be a menorah, a light to the world just as He is. We who believe will not walk in darkness because we now have "the light of life" (John 8:12).

Jesus told a fabulous story to show us how the Holy Spirit is like oil in us that causes us to be a menorah. This is the parable of the Ten Virgins. "At that time the kingdom of heaven will be like ten virgins who took their lamps and went out to meet the bridegroom. Five of them were foolish and five were wise. The foolish ones took their lamps but did not take any oil with them. The wise, however, took oil in jars along with their lamps. The bridegroom was a long time in coming, and they all became drowsy and fell asleep. At midnight the cry rang out: 'Here's the bridegroom! Come out to meet him!' Then all the virgins woke up and trimmed their lamps. The foolish ones said to the wise, 'Give us some of your oil; our lamps are going out.' 'No,' they replied, 'there may not be enough for both us and you. Instead, go to those who sell oil and buy some for yourselves.' But while they were on their way to buy oil, the bridegroom arrived. The virgins who were ready went in with him to the wedding banquet. And the door was shut. Later the others also came. 'Sir! Sir!' they said. "Open the door for us!' But he replied, 'I tell you the truth, I don't know you.' Therefore keep watch, because you do not know the day of the hour (Matthew 25:1-13).

Just as a lamp can't produce light with out the oil to burn in it, a person is not spiritually alive with out the Holy Spirit. In this story, we see that the only way we are prepared for our bridegroom (the end of the age) is to have the oil (The Holy Spirit). Paul says in Romans 8:16, "The Spirit himself testifies with our spirit that we are God's children." And in Ephesians 1:13 Paul says, "And you also were included in Christ when you heard the word of truth, the gospel of your salvation. Having believed, you were marked in Him with a seal, the promised Holy Spirit, who is a deposit guaranteeing our inheritance until the redemption of those who are God's possession to the praise of His glory." The Holy Spirit is the believers, seal, engagement ring, and He is our oil of gladness, and our oil of joy. He the Holy Spirit is the light with in us that enables our light to shine, as in of ourselves all we would be is a candle stick with out a wick and a flame. The Holy Spirit is the pure, clear oil in us that makes us a menorah.

When Jesus walked into Jerusalem for this great Feast of Dedication and celebrated Hanukkah with family and friends, He knew the significance of the lamp that burned for eight days and God's care for His Temple. In a Spiritual way we as believers in Jesus ought to celebrate Jesus as our menorah and know that He can light up our lives with the oil of gladness produced in us by the Holy Spirit. This menorah symbol is a symbol of our true identity in Jesus who brought light to the world. Please don't think this story and symbol is just for cultural Jews. If you believe in Jesus is not your heart circumcised? (Romans 2:17-29). And we are spiritually Jews who are the very children of God by our faith in Jesus the Messiah and the Menorah. If we celebrate Christmas, which is Jesus being birthed into this world, shouldn't we celebrate Jesus being the menorah? And how we too are lights because the Holy Spirit has caused this light to shine in our hearts?[7] And just as the lamp burned miraculously for eight days, give thanks to God that because of this miracle, in our hearts we get to live with God forever.

Jesus said to Peter, "Upon this rock I will build my church" (Matthew 16:18). I believe the rock he was talking about was His identity. It is good and necessary for us to see Jesus as the menorah of the world, the light of life, and the light of our lives. My hope and prayer is that this great story about the miraculous lamp will live again in our hearts and light up our lives. My challenge to you is to retell this great story the next time you enjoy this holiday, and personally "Know-it!", because if you do, you are a bright shining light that this world desperately needs. This too is now your identity.

---

[7] This wonderful "light" theme is more thoroughly developed in **Security from Identity Theft,** Book Three, **Be Light.** Pick it up and see how you can "Be Light!"

Section Two:
NAME IT!

Then Peter said, "Silver or gold I do not have, but what I have I give you. In the name of Jesus Christ of Nazareth, walk.
Acts 3:6

The word from the physical world that can help us secure our identity so that we can "Name-it!" is **Authentication**.

Authentication is the process of verifying a person's identity, and Authorization is the process of verifying that a known person has the authority to perform a certain operation. Authentication must precede Authorization. When we go to our bank we must show the teller our proper identification at this moment we are authenticated when we are approved (He/she matches our face to our Drivers License or identity card and then matches this information to our account information). Now that we are authenticated by the teller we are now authorized to access our account information. We are not authorized to access accounts that we do not own.

Therefore **Authentication** is the use of labels, markings, or special seals which indicate that the package and its contents are authentic. Sometimes people have used fake "IDs" to try to access another person's account. These fake "IDs" have markings on them that pretend to be authentic when in reality they are not. To authenticate a user a teller must do one of the following to authenticate the identity of the user to control their access:

- By asking for something the user has like an ID card, security token, software token, phone or cell phone.
- By asking for something the user knows like passwords, pass codes, pass phrases, or PIN numbers (Personal Identification Numbers)
- Or, by obtaining something the user is or does. They can apply finger print or Retinal (eye) scan, or a DNA sequence, Voice Recognition, or Unique Bio-electrical or Bio-metric identifiers.

From a spiritual standpoint we must know that His (Jesus) name is our name and true identity. The Holy Spirit will bear witness with our human spirit that we truly are a child of God. When this happens in our hearts we are authenticated and truly have security from identity theft. Therefore we "Know-it!", because we have been able to "Name-it!" and now we can access our spiritual accounts and draw upon our great spiritual resources (Romans 8:16).

Something to think about: Because we have been "authenticated" by the Lord Jesus Christ, how can our faith in Him enable us to live authentically? (Think in terms of light, life and love. Do a study of the role of light, life and love in First and Second John. This study is developed for you in Book Four, *All We Need to Know,* to have Security from Identity Theft.)

Chapter 5
LIKE A ROCK STAR

Psalm 18, 40, 27, 61

Today many aspire to live like a rock star! We hear people say things like, "party like a rock star"! "Spend money like a rock star"! He has the popularity of a "rock star"! "I want to live like a rock star"! We seem to covet the identity of a rock star!

In the fall of 2003 I was with my high school golf team at the Pine Creek Golf Course in Colorado Springs. At this particular moment I was wondering through the club house trying to gather my players when I literally bumped into Alice Cooper, you know, of the hit songs WELCOME TO MY NIGHTMARE, SCHOOLS OUT FOR SUMMER *etc*. A real life Rock star! I introduced myself to Alice by saying, "Hello, Alice, I'm Sid Huston and I went to your concert in Omaha in 1975 and I wasn't a Christian at the time." Then Alice stunned me by saying, "I wasn't either". For the next half hour my team gathered around Alice and like a pied piper he enjoyed these guys and told them about his life, his career and his faith in Jesus.

He unreservedly talked about how Jesus has become his life and his true identity. He told us about his struggles with alcohol and how life was like on the road as a rock star. But those famous eyes of his lit up when he began talking about the difference Jesus has made in his life. I was impressed with his humility. He honestly said he didn't know the Bible all that well, but you could tell he was getting real personal with God and was keeping short accounts. He talked about the songs of yesterday, and the new thoughts he was thinking about putting to a beat. He also talked with these young athletes about the benefits of playing golf, and how he liked to integrate his faith, his music, and his golf to help young people. I was really inspired by this time with Alice; we shared the same passions, love for God, love for young people and golf. These were the very reasons I loved coaching these young golfers, walking the fairways and the rough with these guys was the best venue I have found in sports to do evangelism and discipleship.

The next few days at school were a buzz; the hallways were alive with conversation about what these guys heard from Alice Cooper. These guys all loved the Rock n' Roll music of the 60s, 70s, and 80s and here they had just had a moment in time with the legend himself, a real rock star. I bought his latest album and played some of the songs in class (I was a high school Bible teacher) and had some great discussions about his lyrics, his life, and the lessons we learned from him. Every one of my students had a favorite rock star and they loved talking about these people and their lives and how so many ended in tragedy. Alice is one of my favorites because of his transparent faith, and because he has invited me to play golf with him in Phoenix. If anyone knows how to get in touch with him, please let me know. I would like to "tee-it-up" with Alice.

Alice is a good communicator, and he made it clear to all of us that he doesn't know enough to be a spokesman for Jesus, but he also let us know that is not how much you know, but who you know. We were all confident that Alice knew that he knew Jesus Christ personally, and that Jesus was his rock.

There is a "Rock star" in the Bible by the name of David. If David lived today, he would have standing room only crowds at his concerts. Bible lovers everywhere recognize David as one of the most impressive people in all of human history. He was a man of extraordinary talent and heart. He is known as the man after God's own heart. Yet the most telling thing about his life is not his superstar status, but the way he handled his failure. Like most of today's rock stars, this man had a moral failure; it was a humbling and crushing failure, a failure we wouldn't expect from such a wonderful role-model. From David we can learn the power of our true identity and see how a true man of God reacts to failure. It has been said, it is not how we act that shows our true colors, but how we react. David reacted poorly at first and then he realized who God was and who he was in God and things got reconciled. We might be impressed with this rock star for his impressive victories, but we will love him for how he leans into his moral failure. This is a story that gives us hope and perspective, a story that lets us know that what we know will only help so much, but if we know God as our Rock we will be able to overcome.

There is another rock legend from the 70s and the 80s whose music I really like. His name is Bob Seger. I like his ragged and hard driving voice. He wrote a song called *Like a Rock* with words that I believe help us get the rhythm of David's life. I don't think he intentionally planned to do this, but it works. We have all heard this song by watching and listening to the Chevy® truck commercial. The chorus contains these words:

> Like a rock, standin' arrow straight
> Like a rock, chargin' from the gate
> Like a rock carryin' the weight
> Like a rock!

When we look at the life of David we can see him as a young lad standing like a rock. We know him as a boy who was ruddy, he had a fine handsome appearance, and the Lord had anointed him at an early age (1 Samuel 16:12). His father Jessee had him out in the field with the sheep learning great lessons as a young shepherd; can you see him standing out there?

Seger's words help us get the picture:

> Stood there boldly
> Sweatin' in the sun
> Felt like a million
> Felt like number one
> The height of summer
> I'd never felt that strong
> Like a rock.

Even though this young shepherd boy was learning great lessons standing among the sheep, he would be called in to play his harp for King Saul. Word had gotten out that this boy could play. I have loved working Church camps in the summer time, and often in the afternoon free time the kids would gather around the piano and some young guy would work up the courage to step up to the keyboard, and the cronies are dazzled by his skills and by the end of the week this kid is a featured rock star. I imagine in the evening David was "caught" practicing his harp, and in no time the word that this boy can play reached the King. David was then summoned to play for the king, who was being attacked in his human spirit, and David's music would minister to his soul. Now, if we think about it, a harp is a stringed instrument like a guitar. So it really doesn't take much imagination to picture David with the harp on his hip, strumming great cords like a rock star!

Howard Hendricks has said, "If you want to be great with people, you can't always be with people." God had lots of training to do in this anointed young man, and no better place to do it that with the sheep. If you want to read about some of the great lessons David learned as a shepherd, try reading the Twenty Third Psalm. It is a classic! It was during these shepherding days that David was out there "sweatin' in the sun, never felt that strong, like a rock". It was in the fields where he first learned how to trust in God. When a lion or a bear would come and attack his sheep David had to take action. He trusted God to dispatch these predators, and he trusted God to help him develop his marksmanship. He became quite skilled with the slingshot, and he could use the rod like a well trained policeman can use a billy-club. He wasn't just leaning against that staff; this was a salvation stick for him, a real weapon against his enemies. Can you see him standing in the sun, practicing his slingshot, and rehearsing his steps to fend off wild animals with his rod and his staff?

Seger's second verse states:

> I was eighteen,
> Didn't have a care
> Working for peanuts
> Not a dime to spare
> But I was lean and
> Solid everywhere
> Like a rock.

Can you imagine David, as a young shepherd boy out in the fields? And as a young musician practicing his harp? Can you envision him listening to the Holy Spirit and writing poetry that would become the Top 40 play list in the Psalms, which is really a collection of songs? Most of which were written by this rock star. Being out there where he stood boldly, sweatin' in the sun, he fashioned words to songs that have a soul, songs that go deep into our hearts, songs that would be put to a beat and God's children would sing them for thousands of years. Are we impressed yet?

Seger's song has words that describe an event that marked David's life as a rock star forever. This young shepherd boy would one day pick up a rock, not to disperse a predator, but to save his nation from disgrace. This was a point in time event that would settle a dispute and establish him as a legend for the ages. It would also make him despised by King Saul. Because He would be the rock star, and this King an also-ran, a has-been, and yesterday's news. The ladies would sing their own rock n' roll song put to a beat that would make them dance and swoon for David, but it made Saul very angry. The Bible says, "This refrain galled him" (1 Samuel 18:8). The words stated, "Saul has killed his thousands, but David has killed his tens of thousands".

In 1 Samuel 17, Jesse, David's dad, approached him to take some grain and cheese to his brothers who were stationed in the Socoh Valley. Battle lines had been drawn with the Philistines and when David saw his brothers they were trembling with fear. A very intimidating champion from Gath, a real giant of a man was daily taunting the Israeli troops. Goliath would bellow these words, "Choose a man and have him come down to me. If he is able to fight and kill me, we will become your subjects. But if I overcome him and kill him, you will become our subjects and serve us" (1 Samuel 17:8-9). And then the Philistine said, "This day I defy the ranks of the Israel! Give me a man and let us fight each other."

Young David recognized a potential identity theft when he saw one and wasn't going to let God's identity, or the identity of Israel be tarnished. So David ran to the battle lines. He saw Goliath for who he was, an uncircumcised Philistine. In other words he knew this giant was an unholy enemy of God. David, being confident in God's identity and his identity in God, wanted to be the one who would fight and kill this enemy for the Glory of God and secure God's name as the Rock of Israel.

David had to first persuade the leaders to let him face this giant and he did this with practical reasoning and by reminding them how God has delivered him in the past. He made it clear that victories like the won they were about to experience would only be accomplished by faith (Romans 5:1). Then David, with grit and faith, was given the opportunity to confront this enemy and Identity Thief. King Saul tried to get David to wear his heavy armor, but David refused it because it didn't fit, and because this wasn't the identity he was comfortable with. David approached this giant in the Name of almighty God. Even though the giant would shout taunts, and belittle the name of God, David continued to name the name of God and the authority he was in. Even though young David took on this giant wearing only gym shorts and sandals, he was truly wearing the crown, his identity in God, and wielding the scepter of God's authority. The rocks he put in his pouch and the one he put in his slingshot was his weapon of choice, a weapon he was skilled to use, a weapon that was true to his identity.

Seger's Rock N' roll song continues to add music to this drama:

> My hands were steady
> My eyes were clear and bright
> My walk had purpose
> My steps were quick and light
> And I held firmly
> To what I felt was right
> Like a rock!

With one well hurled rock David became a rock star, a legend even to this day. He sized up the giant, he deflected his taunts and insults, he acted out of his identity in God, and this giant fell hard. David took Goliath's sword and cut off his head, and then as he lifted this bloody head, the rout was on. God's people were once again reminded about their identity in God, and the authority that even a boy could rely upon.

Can you hear Seger's chorus?

> Like a rock, I was as strong as I could be
> Like a rock, nothing ever got to me
> Like a rock, I was something to see
> Like a rock.

It was apparent to most that David was a gifted and called man of God. The people were excited for him to be their king. David would become Israel's greatest king. When Jesus came on the scene he would not be called the son of Abraham, or the Son of Jacob. He would be highly esteemed as the Son of David. To the Jew in Israel only Moses is lifted up to the top of this high pedestal.

David's notoriety made King Saul very jealous. And for a very long time David would be running for his life and living as a fugitive. The women sang and danced to that hurtful song with the driving beat, "Saul has killed his thousands, but David has slain his tens of thousands." Unfortunately for David, this song made the hit parade, and David had to run for the hills. This rock star became intimate with the rocks, for they became his shelter, his fortress, his vantage point. No wonder David writes so many songs that depict God as the Rock who saves him; the rocks became his security and friends. Oh, the life of a rock star!

Seger's song has this line in it:

> Of all these hustlers and their schemes
> I stood proud, I stood tall
> High above it all
> I still believed in my dreams.

In my opinion, David wasn't acting proud, but Saul thought he was and that forced David to run to the rock clefts in the mountains. And like a superb song writer, David wrote about the security God provided him with in Psalm 18:

> I love you O LORD, my strength.
> The LORD is my fortress and my deliverer;
> My God is my rock, in whom I take refuge.
> He is my shield and the horn of my salvation,
> My stronghold.
> I call to the LORD, who is worthy of praise,
> And I am saved from my enemies (Psalm 18:1-3).

David found great comfort from God in this rock cave. And God was good to send to David friends to be with him during this time of distress. David's heart was strengthened by God's word, and in knowing that he knows God personally. When you are running for your life, what you know doesn't mean all that much, but who you know can make you secure. David knew God, and he knew God as his rock, therefore David was "like a rock."

David would write:

> With your help I can advance against a troop;
> With my God I can scale a wall.
> As for God, his way is perfect;
> The word of the LORD is flawless.
> He is a shield for all who take refuge in Him.
> For who is God besides the LORD?
> And who is the Rock except our God (Psalm 18:29-32).

For David, God was a rock; He was providing him with security, solid footing, cover, and victory over his enemies.

While in the rock cave at Adullam, David was able to train over 400 warriors, and shape them into a fleet and effective strike force. David was a superb military leader; he was a natural born fighter. I picture him as a William Wallace type we remember in the movie BRAVEHEART, played by Mel Gibson.

During these years David was on the run from Saul's army, David had a couple of opportunities to take Saul's life, but he wouldn't touch the LORD's anointed. He spared Saul's life and showed respect, humility, faith and honor by exercising self control. David even disciplined his troops severely when they had unbridled zeal and stepped over the line. David ruled with integrity and biblical principles.

When King Saul died and David was installed as king, David was only thirty years old. He would reign for forty years and during this time he took control of Jerusalem and it was called the City of David. He built up the area and he became a powerful and righteous king. He knew God had established him for the sake of His people (2 Sam. 5:12). David was also able to capture the Ark of the Covenant and have it restored to Jerusalem. This was a very jubilant and exciting Day for David. The Bible tells us he danced in a very uninhibited way, like a "rock star". Can you imagine him leading the processional and dancing in his "Fruit of the Looms"? So free was he that he embarrassed his wife. David told her that he wasn't dancing for the people, but he was delighting in the Lord. David was a true worshipper, who lived with God alone as his audience.

Seger's song continues:

> Like a Rock, I was strong as I could be
> Like a rock, nothin' ever got to me.
> Like a rock, I was something to see
> Like a Rock!

Like a rock star, David didn't know how to handle his prosperity. He had greatly expanded the kingdom and governed well, but perhaps he had become bored and got too relaxed about his life and his faith. He sent his troops out to war, but this time he stayed home. And instead of living out of his identity as a child of God, David acted like a rock star. He probably felt like he was entitled to some sensual pleasure so he went up on the roof of his palace to do some channel surfing and to gaze upon the women who would be bathing at this time. A beauty named Bathsheba caught his eye and he zoomed in on her, then he summoned for her. He was being driven by his sexual desires, and was attempting to meet his sex need in his own way.

Seger's song plays out:

> And sometimes late at night
> When I'm bathed in the firelight
> The moon comes callin' a ghostly white
> And I recall, I recall.

Like a rock star who plays up to his groupies, David played beautiful Bathsheba. He took advantage of her. What was she to do? He was the King. As a result of this tryst she became pregnant. And like famous rock stars and politicians David shifted into cover-up mode and began to act like an Identity Thief. His first plan was to bring Bathsheba's husband Uriah in from the battle. If he would sleep with her it could possibly cover up this mess. But when Uriah showed up, he was a man of integrity and would only sleep on the porch, because he reasoned "How can I be sleeping with my wife, when my men are in the war?"

David was probably now so guilt ridden that he had Uriah sent back to the battle, and had him assigned to the front lines where his life would surely be cut down. When word got back to David about the battle at the front, and then the message that Uriah had died, David must had descended to the depths of his own depravity as he probably rejoiced that his plan had worked. But, then the LORD sent Nathan the prophet to David. With the courage of a lion and the wisdom of a sage and he told David an identity theft story, a story that got David good and angry (2 Samuel 12). David was so worked up that he said, "The man who performed this identity theft deserves to die." Then with the resolve of a middle linebacker, Nathan said, "You are the man!" David's heart was cut to the core, he was immediately broken when he realized how much God had done for him, yet he had been guilty of great sin, an attempted cover up, and identity theft.

In Psalm 51 we read and experience a depth of brokenness, contrition, and forgiveness that shows us David's heart, and God's mercy. God did blot out David's transgressions and this child that was conceived in sin died. The Bible records the pain David went through as the consequence of his sin, and how he pathetically thought he could cover this with an identity theft. Life can be messy, and yet our great God and King is fully able to take the mess and redeem it. David and Bathsheba did marry, and she conceived and a baby was born to them they named Solomon who would become the wisest man and the richest who ever graced this planet. David would be happy to know that his throne was firmly established under Solomon's leadership. And the world is blessed with the finest wisdom literature, and scriptures that put life in perspective from Solomon's pen. Check out the book of Ecclesiastes, Song of Solomon and some of the Proverbs of Solomon to gain wisdom insights from this Son of David, this child of grace, this man who also knew that what really matters in life is knowing God (Read Ecc. 12).

David had another son, who, like Saul, made him run for his life. His name was Absalom. Absalom was power hungry and he had conspired to steal power away from Daddy David. But Absalom's attempts to honor himself, and establish his own kingdom were foiled. He ended up dying in a very unusual way. While riding on a mule he went under the branches of a large oak tree, and his big head got caught in the tree and he was left hanging in midair (2 Samuel 18). The mule couldn't even stand this guy and it just kept going and Absalom was left hanging. Joab, a military man, took three javelins and plunged them into Absalom's heart while he was still alive and hanging in the tree. Then Joab's armor bearers struck and killed him, they then threw him into a pit and piled up rocks on him. That's a different kind of rock story about a man who was anything but a rock star.

David before he died was able to install Solomon as King of Israel. He gave him a charge that emboldened him in his true identity in God, a charge that every dad should give to his sons. He said, "So be strong, show yourself a man, and observe what the LORD your God requires; walk in His ways, and keep His decrees and commands, His laws and requirements, as written in the laws of Moses, so that you may prosper in all you do and wherever you go" (1 Kings 2:3-4). David then died, after living a full life and fully realizing the authority of the name of God. He knew God as a rock, and he also showed by his failure and contrition the mercy and grace of God.

Seger's song continues:

> Twenty years now
> Where'd they go?
> Twenty years
> I don't know
> I sit and wonder sometimes
> Where they've gone.

David knew God as his rock, and even in the insecure times he learned to trust that in Him he would be secure. He wrote a rock song we call Psalm 40:

> I waited patiently for the LORD;
> He turned to me and heard my cry.
> He lifted me out of the slimy pit,
> Out of the mud and mire;
> He set my feet on a rock and gave me
>   a firm place to stand.
> He put a new song in my mouth, a hymn
>   of praise to our God (Psalm 40:1-3).

I don't know what Bob Seger used to get his inspiration for this song, maybe it is just coincidence that it can be used to reflect upon David's life, or for that matter our own. But, as you think of King David, can you hear David say, "Like a rock, God is my Rock, He makes me stand secure, and He is my Rock"?

Listen to a couple of David's greatest hits: (read them out loud for effect!)

In Psalm 61 we read:

> Hear my cry, O God;
> Listen to my prayer,
> From the ends of the earth
> I call to you,
> I call as my heart grows faint;
> Lead me to the rock that is higher than I.

For you have been my refuge,
A strong tower against the foe.
I long to dwell in your tent forever
And take refuge in the shelter of your wings
(Psalm 61:1-4).

These are the lyrics of a real rock star, and now that we have lived in his story for just a bit, we see why he knew God his Rock. In Psalm 27:1-5 we are privileged to listen to a classic:

The LORD is my light and my salvation—
Whom shall I fear?
The LORD is the stronghold of my life—
Of whom shall I be afraid?
When evil men advance against me
To devour my flesh,
When my enemies and my foes attack me,
They will stumble and fall.
Though and army besiege me,
My heart will not fear;
Though war break out against me,
My heart will not fear,
Even then will I be confident.
One thing I ask of the LORD,
This is what I seek:
That I may dwell in the house of the LORD
All the days of my life,
To gaze upon the beauty of the LORD
And to seek Him in His temple.
For in the day of trouble
He will keep me safe in His dwelling;
He will hide me in the shelter
Of His tabernacle and set me high upon
A rock
(Psalm 27:1-5).

We can be like a Rock:

Like a rock, the sun upon my skin
Like a rock, hard against the wind
Like a rock, I see myself again
Like a rock.

David is the rock star of Israel because he knew God by name, he knew Him as his rock! We too can live like a rock star, not the look at me type, but we can be like David who humbly experienced the heights and the depths and found that God was his rock. Like David knew God, we too can humbly name His name and by faith know that He is our Rock. By knowing God as our Rock, we can live securely, "like a rock", and have security from identity theft.

Chapter 6
GREAT FAKE OUTS

Mark 4

There are only a handful of athletes that I would pay money to watch compete. Every time I have the opportunity to watch Tiger Woods play golf, I will try to see him. I believe he is the greatest athlete I will ever see in my lifetime. I think Michael Jordan was a phenomenal basketball player; his unusual athleticism and competitive spirit were something special to behold. Then there was Barry Sanders. I just loved watching this guy run with the football. I believe Barry would have been a scary player to defend because you always had the feeling he could score from anywhere. Today I would hate to have to guard Allen Iverson of the Denver Nuggets. He is a threat anywhere on the basketball court. The Phoenix Suns have a fabulous playmaking point guard on their basketball team named Steve Nash. He is a thrill a minute type of player who is fun to watch. But, the athlete I have watched over and over again is Pistol Pete Maravich. I have a copy of his LSU (Louisiana State University). highlight film and I have worn it out. Pete was for sure the greatest college basketball player I have ever seen, and his statistics bear it out.

The Pistol was a scoring machine for the LSU Tigers (NCAA-college), and to my surprise he wasn't the quickest or the fastest player I'd ever seen lace up his "Pro Keds" basketball shoes and flop his socks (Pete was known for wearing floppy socks). Pete's college highlight film is a classic study in ball handling, passing and shooting, but I have watched how he sets up his legendary moves with great fakes. Just a little hesitation here, or a jab step there, he will pull his arm one way, and then throw the ball with the other and make his opponent look silly as he hoists another jump shot for two points. Pete didn't need to put his defender into the stands with a cheap shot or a push, just a little muscle twitch and he had the two inches of extra space he needed to pull-up and smooth another jumper. His opponents had to respect his moves because he could beat you with his triple threat. In a split second he would burn his opponent with his deadly accurate jump shot, a behind the back pass, or amazing dribble- drive to the hoop.

Pete was such a prolific scorer in the college game that he scored over fifty points twenty eight times, he averaged over forty-four points per game and experts think he would have averaged more than fifty points per game if they would have had the three point line back in the day. Pete was not the slam dunker and high flying circus acts you see so many ball players trying to be today. He was a pure shooter, pure passer and a pure ball handler and to do all these parts of the game well, he implemented fakes to set up his moves like a magician. Pete is regarded as the greatest college player of all time and was a five time NBA all-star; in 1977 he led the NBA with a 31 points per game scoring average.

"Pistol" Pete is a classic study in identity theft. Pete did not like the tag "Pistol" that a local sports writer labeled him with, but it stuck. He didn't like it because he didn't want to be known as a "gunner", a player who selfishly shot the ball when teammates were open. He didn't want to be known as a glory hog, he wanted to be known as a team player, it is just that he had a gift to score with the ball and his team mates enjoyed feeding this machine. He kept them awake. Often his teammates were so mesmerized by his magical style of play that they would get caught spectating, just watching, and then Pete would zip a pass right to them. If they weren't ready it might hit them on their nose.

Like most Dads who live vicariously through their son's success, Pete's dad, Press Maravich was a former professional basketball player and coach. When Pete was at LSU he played for his dad, and Press was overzealous about his son's abilities. Press would brag to the media about his son's performances and everyone could tell that Dad's hype made things even tougher on Pete, not to mention the weight of being called the "Pistol." Pete had a good relationship with his dad, they spent lots of time together, but most of it was around basketball, and this relationship sadly gave the Identity Thief some room to steal Pete's true identity away. Instead of learning from his dad the lessons of character from the scriptures, and his proper identity in God, Press pushed Pete to become an icon, an identity he would resent. This identity of "the Pistol" made life tough for Pete, and even contributed to a depression that prompted some illicit and damaging behaviors.

Here was one of the greatest basketball players of all time, and one of the few players I would actually pay to watch play, a true superstar, but he was far from being a super-star person. Even though he had the one point six million dollar contract, the envious basketball skills, the television commercials that featured "Pistol Pete", and his outrageous statistics, Pete became a recluse. Here he had all the trappings this world could put out, yet nothing brought Pete a sense of purpose or a belief that his life was significant.

A leg injury forced Pete to go on a two year search for meaning. He tried everything, and he was like Solomon who tried it all and realized that everything was vanity and chasing after the wind (Ecclesiastes 4:6). Pete looked to religions like Hinduism and the practice of yoga, UFOs, and even vegetarianism and studies in macrobiotics. This was a weird and desperate search for his true identity. He knew that being "Pistol Pete" wasn't enough, and then he became a follower of Jesus Christ. This belief in Jesus so transformed his life that he knew he had found his true identity. Maravich said, "I want to be remembered as a Christian, a person that serves him to the utmost. Not as a basketball player."

While watching some of my video of Pete, I noticed that even when he was being fouled and knocked out of bounds while shooting the basketball, Pete kept his eye on the rim. No wonder so many of his shots went in. He trained himself to not take his eye off the goal, and he scored many three point plays because of this unusual ability to focus. When Pete started living for Jesus this attitude of focusing on Jesus, the goal of his life, was an inspiration to everyone who knew Pete.

At the young age of forty, Pete died suddenly while warming up to scrimmage with Dr. James Dobson and associates who loved to play basketball at Focus on the Family. This was supposed to be a happy day for all involved, and in a spiritual way it was. Come to find out, Pete had accomplished all his great athletic exploits with only one coronary artery instead of two; consequently he had an over sized and over worked heart. The Identity Thief didn't get a victory here as Pete's story about his search and his true faith and identity transformation has reached out to millions of people through the assistance of Christian athletes and ministries like Focus on the Family.

Just as a basketball player learns to fake-out his opponent to take advantage of them, the devil is an Identity Thief who has mastered great fakes to exploit his opponents. In Mark chapter 4:3-8, Jesus tells a parable that explains all the parables he would tell the world. In this parable of the sower, He presents a vivid word picture that shows how the Identity Thief has mastered great fake-outs to mislead the masses. He says, "Listen! A farmer went out to sow his seed, some fell along the path, and the birds came and ate it up. Some fell on rocky places, where it did not have much soil. It sprang up quickly because the soil was shallow. But when the sun came up, the plants were scorched, and they withered because they had no root. Other seed fell among thorns, which grew up and choked the plants, so that they did not bear grain. Still other seed fell on good soil. It came up, grew and produced a crop, multiplying thirty, sixty, or even a hundred times."

Only Jesus could defend against this fake-out artist, He knows the Identity Thief's strategies and in this text he reveals his moves. He explains that the seed is the Word of God, and the Identity Thief gets the seed to fall on hard packed path's and then like a vulture he swoops in and devours the seed. That is his first fake-out, he gets the seed to fall on hard hearts and then he dives in and steals the seed like a basketball defender would steal a pass. This fake-out makes it so the seed doesn't have a chance to grow, a person can't be transformed and the thief is happy about his moves.

The thief's second fake is to get the seed to fall on to a rocky yard kind of heart. The thief gives them short term happiness but does not allow them to develop roots, so that when trouble, temptations and persecutions come they quickly wither like a weed sprayed with "weed-be-gone." And his last fake-out occurs when he can get the seed to fall among the weeds. Jesus tells us that the weeds are the worries of the world and the deceptiveness of riches.

For the longest time Pistol Pete had been faked out by this scheme. He had heard the Word of God, but in spite of his million dollar contract, and his super star status, he didn't have peace in his heart. I remember watching him play as a pro and there were games he looked like a zombie out on the court, a life-less performer on auto pilot, no-heart, no passion, no fire in his belly. He looked worried and unhappy because he was. The Identity Thief had turned the Pistol on the Pistol and now he was shooting himself in his own foot. Everyone seemed to be critical of Pete, the coaches, sports writers and the fans. One sports writes said there wasn't enough mustard to put on that hotdog, referring to Pete. This was terribly frustrating time for Pete, to be caught in the middle of the Identity Thief's warfare, with out an understanding of how to win this war within, being with out God and without hope.

We see three specific fake-out moves the Identity Thief uses. The first is to get people to devalue the Word of God, get them to think that it is irrelevant, unscientific and boring, and get them to believe anything for the sake of preventing the reading of it. Secondly he fakes people out with happiness. He allows people to perceive the Word of God, but prevents them from growing their roots into God by making sure their hearts are like a rocky yard. These lives are quickly sun-scorched and quickly blown away.

Lastly he gets people to think that they are happy and growing only to perform a sneaky choke hold on them to prevent them from becoming alive in God. He works with the worlds systems, and causes many concerns to put people in a death grip. I've seen this move a thousand times, how many young men were hearing the Word of God and then they got a car. Car-fever (or technology fever) begins to consume their time and their minds and they are caught up in their stuff and any spiritual life is choked out because they are distracted and never got established in the Word of God. I've seen many young ladies pick up a Brides magazine, fall in love with the idea of being in love and get all lathered up in make-up, hair styles and clothes. This passion for a guy or for status might make these girls look pretty on the outside, they might even regularly attend church, but inwardly they are worldly and spiritually dead. I have actually seen young ladies who are more in love with the idea of being a bride than with the man they are going to marry. In a spiritual way the Identity Thief gets us to focus on the wrong things, so we stumble over his fake out moves.

In my twenty five years of pastoral ministry I could tell many stories about people I dearly love who have stumbled for each of these three fake out moves the Identity Thief puts on them. The sad reality here is that these great fake out moves not only impact the individual who got faked out but in some cases an entire community, a Church, school or youth group got faked out. And just as we have often seen a defender land on his keister because he or she got faked out, we have all stumbled because of one of these great fake outs.

Let's take a look at Coach Tate Almond (Not his real name, but he is a real nut!). This guy was a famous high school football coach. He was a terrific motivator and the boys who played for him played at a very high level. Coach Almond would roam the sidelines with his ten gallon cowboy hat and cowboy boots. When his team would score that hat would be sailing high into the bright Friday night lights. Too bad this old coach fell prey to the Identity Thief's bait; he was baited with the thought that he should have more money in his pocket than he was making coaching. So when coach Almond was propositioned to use his people skills to arrange a couple of drug deals he thought he deserved the thousands of dollars that would fill his pocket.

I met this old coach after he got caught and had done some prison time. I was more than happy to try to help rehab this football legend. He seemed to receive the Word of God with eagerness, and he was quick to integrate God into his conversations with people who asked him how he was doing. I had honest and convicting conversations with this old coach and he always gave me the right answers. But, his love for the bright lights and the big deal was catching up with him. One day I needed him to pick up breakfast as I didn't have enough money in my pocket, and why should I buy all the meals anyway? When I made him dig into his pocket I observed a large wad of one hundred dollar bills. This amount of money must have been the payoff of another drug deal. I knew then that this was just another jail house conversion, and that this dog had returned to his vomit. I sincerely regretted the way I had been faked out and used by

Coach Almond to hide behind my ministry. I know the good seed of the Gospel had been cast to his soul like a quarterback throws the ball to a wide receiver, but the old coach didn't catch it. I believe he was nothing more than a hard-packed heart and the Identity Thief intercepted the good seed that was sown right off his finger tips, and he never did partake of the life of Jesus. I sincerely do hope this story will someday have a better ending.

Then there was "Rocky Nameth" (not his real name) who was a star high school quarterback. When Rocky came to college where I was serving as a youth and college pastor he was having a serious identity challenge. You see, he had been the star Q.B. in high school and he just assumed he would make the college team and keep on marching in the look at me parade. Rocky was having an identity crisis but he didn't know it. The Identity Thief had helped him become depressed by constantly reminding him that he was now no longer a football hero, but rather nothing but a zero because he failed to make the team. This is when I met Rocky and got him involved in Bible study on the college campus. He was happy to be invited to the group and I assumed the Bible study was having an impact because we met at 7:00am in the morning and attendance was a real sacrifice for most of the college students. I really thought Rocky was a growing Christian so I challenged him to become a summer intern and work with our high school students on a summer ministry project. He loved the idea, and stepped right up to the challenge. The students loved him, he was a natural leader, and had great report with the kids. They especially loved playing football with Rocky; I thought for sure God was redeeming his experience.

But, as soon as a conflict arose in the group, Rocky's enthusiasm for Jesus, the Bible and ministry vanished. I believe some of Rocky's old football buddies got to him. I think as they began to mock his new faith, his new lifestyle and his new friends, he couldn't take it and he quit. Yes, right in the middle of our summer ministry project Rocky abandoned us. I tried to chase him down, and give him the old rah, rah, to rejuvenate him but the Identity Thief had already stolen the seed. The sad reality for me was the revelation that Rocky really didn't have life in him, no roots, and there was no SAP (The

Spirit and the Anointing is released by Praise) flowing in his body so when the hot dry winds of discouragement and conflict blew towards Rocky he was gone with the wind, and there I stood. My head was like it was on a swivel I was so faked out.

With tears I must tell you the story of Dustin Timberlake (not his real name, but he could have been a "Mousesketeer"). Dustin was a handsome young guy, and he was a very likeable. Every one talked about his enthusiasm and energy. And besides this, he was brimming with musical talent, and he seemed totally committed to Jesus. Dustin quickly became one of our student leaders and during his time with us our ministry flourished. This was during a season of ministry where these students not only reached out to hundreds of their friends but they made Jesus a natural topic of conversation on their high school campus. I poured lots of time into Dustin and he seemed to really appreciate it, and it looked like he was sincerely trying to apply God's Word to his life. I thought for sure Dustin was a "FATER" young man. I always used acrostics to teach and this stood for: Faithful, Available, Teachable, Enthusiastic, and Responsible, he seemed to fit the description. Looking back I think the problem started with Dustin's broken home, his parents had been divorced and Dustin never really believed he was accepted by his new mom. There might have even been abuse here, but Dustin never talked with me about it. So when Dustin came to church he literally raced to the youth group to find refuge. We provided Dustin lots of places to hide his real pain; he was a talented singer and actor. But looking back I can now see that he just really loved the spotlight and the applause the church family gave him. The church seemed to fill his "love-bucket" but as soon as he graduated from high school and his friends went away to college Dustin felt like he was dust in the wind. He felt abandoned because he was not financially able to pursue his music and acting dreams at the college level. Soon the worries of the world and the deceitfulness of riches gave him a big head fake.

It wasn't long before homosexual men began to entice young Dustin. All they had to do was appeal to his talent and his good looks and he would fall as their prey. The Identity Thief used these men to entice him with money and false security. Before long Dustin was trading sexual favors for money and lodging. And today he has HIV AIDs and no longer has the strength to stand and sing. The Identity Thief has accomplished and amazing fake out. I thought for sure Dustin was a Spirit filled and joyous follower of Jesus. But, come to find out, Dustin never found his identity in Jesus, he was only finding his identity in his body, his singing and his relationships. As I look back at this tragedy I feel terrible for Dustin, I wish I could have done more, but I was faked out, I guess I didn't go deep enough in my ministry to Dustin, I am so sorry about being to superficial. I pray for God to heal him physically and spiritually. I can't imagine how painful this has been for Dustin, to see the weeds of this world put a stranglehold on him and choke him to death. I hope he finds true life in Jesus before this disease eats away his body.

It is painful for me to admit that I have gone for many of the Identity Thief's fakes. I have fallen to my knees because I have been humbled by hard hearted fakes, rocky hearted fakes, and weedy heart fakes. And the painful truth of the matter is that these are people I have loved with all my heart. But, like a basketball player trying to defend against Pistol Pete Maravich, there are days I find myself jumping into the bleachers having gone for one of his well executed fakes. The thing I have been humbled by is the reality of true and false conversions. I have seen a number of false conversions and now I no longer tell somebody that they are a Child of God just because they prayed a little prayer with me. I wait and let the Holy Spirit give them the witness of His presence in their lives and when I see real fruit and we have true fellowship then we celebrate the reality of a true conversion together.[8]

My joy is being hated by the Identity Thief! Think about it, the more I learn about the role of God's law in bringing people to Jesus, and the rule of God's grace in the hearts of people the more effective I become. And the more effective I become the more hated I am by the Identity Thief. This is why it is so important for us to draw our sense of identity completely from Jesus and not from other people. When our eyes are on people it is easy to get faked out. The way to reduce the

---

[8] See Appendix #1, "Pyramid to Victory" on page 219.

number of times we get faked out is to focus on pleasing Jesus and quit being a people pleaser. When bank tellers are trained to identify counterfeit money they are trained to see what the characteristics are of true money. This way when a false or counterfeit bill passes their eye they can spot it in an instant. This is what we must do if we don't want to take the Identity Thief's fakes, get to know Jesus so well that we know His heart, His character, His personality, and His fruit. Only then will we be able to keep our feet and really stand during the competition for souls of men and women and boys and girls. By knowing the difference between true and false conversions, and by learning how to detect his great fakes, we can have security from identity theft and be "like a rock."

Chapter 7
GOD'S JEHOVAH NAMES

Proverbs 18:10

The name of the LORD is a strong tower; the
righteous run to it and are safe.

There are three things we need to know about God.

#1. He is God.
#2. We are not Him.
#3. Our lives become secure and purposeful by
knowing Him in His Jehovah names.

John the beloved disciple understood the importance of
applying God's name to our own lives. He said, "Yet to all who
received Him, to those who believed in His name. He gave the right to
become children of God—children born not of natural descent, not of
human decision of a husbands will, but born of God" (John 1:12-13).

Having a great father can make a huge impact on a person's
life. I know a man who has adopted children from the corners of the
world, and he owns an amusement park with go-carts, laser tag, and
lots of cool games. Those kids are going to have a blast growing up,
and the coolest thing is this Dad just loves to play with his children at
his amusement park.

Not everyone is blessed with a hip "earthly" father, but by
grace we can all be received into our Heavenly Father's family and
begin to appropriate all the benefits of His names. Sadly, most
Christian people do not know much about their Heavenly Father,
because they have not had the opportunity to learn about His
"Jehovah" names. When we learn about these names, we can then
focus on applying the benefit of each of these names to our own lives.

I remember a guy I went to college with whose Dad had great
cars, money, and owned neat vacation spots. He even had a good
personality, and loved his son, but for some strange reason this buddy

of mine never wanted to hang out with his dad, and get to know all the ways his dad wanted to bless him.

Early in the history of Israel God let His people know His name, but because the scribes were so reverent with how they wrote it, they chose to never write it out completely. The result of this reverent act is that we now don't exactly know His name because all they left for us were four English letters JHVH or the equivalent Hebrew letters YHWH. Over the years names came from these letters, Jehovah and Yahweh.

The most famous way God has identified Himself is as "I AM". He told Moses in Exodus 3:14, "I am who I am." And sent Moses off to speak with the Egyptian Pharaoh and set His people free. Moses went in God's name, and this serves as our example to live out of His names too.

By saying He is "I Am"; He is saying He is the self-becoming one, the unchanging one, the self sustaining one, the incomprehensible one. Just as God is infinite, He is also personal. But, so what? If we don't know Him personally, and learn to appropriate the power and the authority of His names, it would be like Donald Trump's children never learning their last name. They would never fly in the Trump helicopter, play on the Trump golf courses, or live in the Trump towers. How silly it would be for Donald Trump's children to live on the streets or become wards of the state when their dad is Donald Trump!

JEHOVAH-JIREH

Throughout the Old Testament God extends to us His Jehovah names by revealing them to us through His actions. I will tell you some of the stories and how God used these experiences to introduce us to His Jehovah names. It starts in Genesis 22:14 when God shows Abraham that He is Jehovah *Jireh*—the God who sees, and that He is the God who provides.

Satan the Identity Thief always brings temptations, but God always brings testings to strengthen our faith. God appeared to Abraham by saying, "Abraham", "Here I am." And then He asked Abraham to take this son he loved, this special son of promise, the son of his old age, this son named Isaac and take him to Moriah and sacrifice him on the mount. Abraham obeyed God and walked up that mountain by faith with his son and the supplies needed to make this sacrifice to God.

I can only imagine the emotion in the conversation this dad was having with his son on this hike. And as they hiked and talked about making a sacrifice to God, this son was probably taking inventory of their supplies. Isaac was carrying the wood, and Abraham was packing the knife and the fire. Then Isaac asked, "Where is the sacrifice?" Abraham responded in a way that gives us God's first Jehovah name. He says, "God will provide". In the original language he is calling God, Jehovah *Jireh*—the God who sees, and the God who provides.

Abraham took God at is word and obediently laid Isaac out on the makeshift altar, and as Abraham was grabbing for the knife to obey God, the angel of God called out and called off this sacrifice because Jehovah *Jireh*—had provided another.

God is true to His name, and Jehovah *Jireh* had placed a ram in the thicket, one that had already been caught by its horns. This became a suitable sacrifice and a marvelous provision that helps us to see that God sees ahead, and that God provides in advance. I believe He had this ram there even before Abraham and Isaac made their long hike up the mount to obey God in what He asked.

We are challenged like Abraham to know God as Jehovah *Jireh*. I believe the Apostle Paul was referring to Abraham's example when he compared God's sacrifice of His Son and told us how God is intent on providing for us. He said, "He who did not spare His own Son, but gave Him up for us all—how will He not also with Him graciously give us all things" (Romans 8:32).

Knowing God by His Jehovah *Jireh* name means that we can personally know that, "My God will meet all your needs according to His glorious riches in Christ Jesus" (Phil 4:19). He is the God who sees ahead of us, and is faithful and able to provide all our needs. He is the God who lacks nothing.

Satan, the Identity Thief, will work to cause us to doubt these truths about His name. He will try to distort our thinking and defraud us of the blessings of believing in God's promises (Hebrews 11:6). God has promised to open the windows of heaven and pour out blessings on us; yet Satan will try to keep us from looking up and seeing these open windows.

JEHOVAH-ROPHE

Moses met with God at the burning bush, where he received instructions to return with Aaron to Egypt and confront Pharaoh to "let my people go" after God caused many creative and convincing plagues, plagues of blood, frogs, flies, gnats, livestock, boils, hail, locusts, darkness and ultimately the plague on the firstborn. It wasn't till this last plague that the hard hearted Pharaoh relented and let God's children go.

God miraculously saved his people with the blood of a lamb on their door posts, and when death "passed over" these blood protected people, an exodus began like a huge parade. There were God's fruitful people and their animals and what few possessions they had making this huge national hike we call the Exodus. As they were approaching the Red Sea, these travelers took a look in their rearview mirror and noticed a hard charging Egyptian army coming after them. At this sighting the grumbling began. They complained to Moses and accused him of bringing them out into the desert to die. Why do we think our faith shouldn't be tested daily?

With their backs to Egypt and their face fronting the Red Sea, they saw God pull off a miracle. He parted the waters and all of God's children walked across on dry ground, with the waters piled up in a heap, they were able to watch the Egyptian chariots and their riders drive into the sea area only to see God pull the plug on these warriors and drown them in a tidal wave of water. This must have inspired praise and applause, more than any roar you would hear at a football game, because this was a great miracle.

As they continued their travel to the Promised Land, and trekking through the desert they quickly forgot to praise God as their mouths were dry with thirst. They began to grumble and their volume increased as they came to Marah where there was water but it was bitter. Moses cried out to the Lord and the Lord showed him a piece of

wood that he would plop into the water. And like the old Alka seltzer®
commercia, "plop, plop, fizz, fizz, oh what a relief it is!" The bitter
water instantly became sweet and pure. It was at this point in time that
God revealed Himself to His people as Jehovah *Rophe*-the God who
heals.

Through Jesus we see God as our Jehovah *Rophe* as He heals
us with the wood of the cross He died on. Peter Said, "He Himself
bore our sins on His body on the tree, so that we might die to sins and
live for Righteousness, for by His wounds you have been healed" (1
Peter 2:24).

Many people today ask, can God or Does God heal today? I
simply respond by stating that God is the same today as He was
yesterday, and He will be the same forever. He is the God who heals,
He is our Jehovah *Jireh*. He can heal physical ailments, emotional
confusion, broken relationships, and a mean or evil human spirit.

The Identity Thief will be on the prowl, and will try to
influence us to grumble and complain instead of believing in him for a
healing. Grumbling and complaining attitudes are the opposite of faith,
they are inconsistent with our identity in Jehovah *Rophe*-the God who
heals (Read Phil. 2:14).

The medical profession has the most unusual symbol to
communicate healing; it is a snake on a stick. Perhaps you have seen
this and wondered what in the world is this? Moses had to deal with
lots of grumbling people, and God was so tired of this so He sent
venomous snakes that bit these people. I think I would have done the
same thing. The people then came to Moses and were now confessing
their sins, and pleading with God to take these snakes away and to heal
them. So Moses placed a bronze snake on a pole, a symbol of that
which was killing them became the power which would heal them, the
snake was lifted up and the people looked up to it and were healed.

JEHOVAH-NISSI

That symbol became a Banner, a preview of the cross Jesus
would die on and a picture of how a symbol of death becomes a
statement of life to us. Just as the cross means death but to those of us
who look up and believe, it becomes life to us. In John 3:14 we are

told that Jesus would be lifted up just like the bronze serpent in the wilderness. He became sin so that by faith when we look to Him and believe we become the very righteousness of God (2 Cor. 5:21). A figure of defeat becomes our victory banner, and now we can know God as Jehovah-*Nissi*-our God our victory Banner!

God revealed this name to us in Exodus 17 where Joshua followed Moses' commands and fought the Amalekites. This was an overwhelming battle, so Moses went to the top of a hill and held up his hands to God. As his hands remained up God's children were winning the battle. But, after fatigue set in and his hands were lowered the battle turned to the Amalekites. So Aaron and Hur came alongside Moses and held his hands up. And as his hands were lifted Joshua and the fighting men were able to overcome the Amalakite Army. In remembrance of this victory, Moses built an altar to God and called it, "the LORD my banner." Jehovah-*Nissi*!

We too should thank God for being our Jehovah-*Nissi*, because now we know that victory is certain in Jesus who is our "Jehovah-Savior", this is what the name Jesus means. The apostle Paul said, "But thanks be to God! He gives us the victory through our Lord Jesus Christ. Therefore, my dear brothers, stand firm, let nothing move you, always give yourselves fully to the work of the Lord, because you know that your labor in the lord is not in vain" (1 Cor. 15:57-58).

JEHOVAH-MEKEDDESHEM

Many years ago now I was mentored by a great old football coach named Dan Stavely. Coach would tell me, "keep your heart pure and you will have the strength of ten men." Then he would talk about how metal is made strong, he would say you have to remove the dross. The dross is all the impurities, and what is true of metal is also true of men, remove that which is impure and we become strong.

In Leviticus 20:7-8 God calls himself Jehovah-*Mekeddshem* the LORD who sanctifies. This means He is the one who makes us holy! For some worldly reasons Moses was having great difficulty keeping God's children from following Molech. Molech's followers would consult mediums, and engage in spiritism this seemed to be a more sensational spiritual life to God's children and they were drawn to this. They chose the gods of this world over the "ho hum" Jehovah-*Mekeddeshem* the God who sanctifies. This worlds glitz and glamour has always been an idol God's people have difficulty resisting.

So, God said to Moses, "consecrate yourselves and be holy, because I am the LORD your God. Keep my decrees and follow them. I am the one who makes you holy." Sanctification is the spiritual process whereby God aligns our behavior to be consistent with our true identity in Him. He is our Jehovah-*Mekeddeshem*, the God who makes us holy!

Sanctification is both a position and a process. When we are born again by the Holy Spirit the moment we place our faith in Jesus, in that moment we are positionally sanctified. This means we were made new, we became a new creation (2 Cor. 5:17) and were given new hearts. And God the Father now sees us as holy and acceptable to Him and at the same time begins the practical and necessary process of transforming us into the likeness of Jesus. Paul wrote to the church at Corinth and said, "To the church of God in Corinth, to those sanctified in Christ Jesus and called to be holy, together with all those everywhere who call on the name of our Lord Jesus Christ- their Lord and ours: Grace and peace to you from God our Father and the Lord Jesus Christ" (I Corinthians. 1:2).

The reason I point out this interesting text, is because it shows that believers in Jesus are seen as being (past tense) sanctified in Christ, and yet there is still a future and continuous work of sanctification to be done. The text says we are called to be holy, so we are holy in our position "in Christ", and yet like a slab of marble that is being chiseled into a beautiful image, there is a lot of material being removed from our lives until we are like Him. This is a painful process where we struggle to let go of sins, but it is a beautiful process and we become more like Jesus every day.

Paul knew Jehovah-*Mekeddeshem* and he said, "It is God's will that you should be sanctified: that each of you should avoid sexual immorality; that each of you should learn to control his own body in a way that is holy and honorable, not is passionate lust like the heathen, who do not know God" (1Thessalonians 4:4-5).

Certainly the Identity Thief will work to prevent this type of identity alignment from happening, as he wants us to be like him and not like Jesus. God is Jehovah-*M'Kaddesh*, the God who makes us holy!

JEHOVAH-SHALOM

Romans 5:1-2 pulls some of these same great truths together, the truths about faith, grace, righteousness and peace. It says, "Therefore, since we have been justified through faith, we have peace with God through our Lord Jesus Christ, through whom we have gained access by faith into this grace in which we now stand."

Gideon is known as a mighty warrior who would take on the Midianites with a reduced army of 300 men. What many don't realize is that he desperately needed God's peace. In Judges 6:24 we see when Gideon came to know God as Jehovah-*Shalom*, the God of peace. Many Bible scholars believe Jesus appeared to Gideon as an angel, and explained to him how he would lead Israel to overcome the oppression of the Midianites. But, Gideon was very afraid and this angel introduced himself by saying, "Peace! Do not be afraid." This is a similar introduction Jesus would make as he greeted His disciples, and he would often say, "Take courage it is I, don't be afraid" (Mark 6:50).

Gideon took this special angel at His word, believed God, and experienced peace. In response to this peace he built an altar for God and called it, "The LORD is peace-Jehovah *Shalom.*

The life of Gideon parallels ours; his circumstances were not conducive for peace. Even as I write this book I struggle with peace as my circumstances are tough. At present I am not employed, my kids are in college, I don't have any guarantees, my cars are wearing out and so is my body, and I don't know how I am going to pay for any of it, car repairs or medical bills.

Gideon's back was against the wall, he was stressed by the overwhelming force of the Midianites, and his army was small, yet the Lord was his peace. In this account we learn that peace is not the absence of conflict, but the presence of God. The Identity Thief plays to our doubts and our fears; he plays these two like a broken record, over and over again. He does this to get us to look to everything other than God, he will even introduce us to temporary escapes like, drugs, sex, entertainment, that will give us a bit of an adrenaline rush to mask our fears, but this is nothing like the peace of God.

Jesus said, "Peace I leave with you; my peace I give you. I do not give to you as the world gives. Do not let your hearts be troubled and do not be afraid" (John 14:27). Jesus shows us Jehovah-*Shalom*, as he gives us peace, a peace that surpasses comprehension, and nothing in this world comes close to this bless gift of comforting peace (Phillipeans 4:6-7).

JEHOVAH-ROHI

David the great king was once a shepherd boy and he wrote a Psalm from a sheep's perspective. It is the most loved Psalm of all, the Twenty third Psalm. In it he said, "The LORD is my shepherd, I shall not be in want. He makes me lie down in green pastures, He leads me beside quiet waters, He restores my soul" (Psalm 23:1-3). In this peaceful picture David learned that a sheep was totally dependent on the shepherd for peace. It is the shepherd who guides, protects and provides for all the sheep's needs. Therefore, even though the sheep has to walk through the valley of death, and is like a fat meal being set before its enemies, the sheep choose not to fear for they have learned and gained confidence in the skills and the care of their shepherd. The little sheep turn their beady eyes to the shepherd there leaning on his staff and they know they will be protected by his rod, and they are comforted, and they learn that he is their peace. David said here in this Psalm that God is Jehovah-*Rohi,* the LORD is our shepherd.

In the New Testament Gospel of John chapter 10, Jesus shows himself as our Jehovah-*Rohi* as He says, "I am the good Shepherd, the Good Shepherd lays down his life for the sheep" (John 10:11). In this chapter Jesus shows how He, Jehovah-*Rohi*, knows the sheep, (3 & 14) owns the sheep, (12) stays with the sheep, and even promises to go after them when they stray. Sheep are prone to wonder, but we are blessed to have a Good Shepherd who will risk His life for us and pursue us. Satan the Identity Thief will try to get us to think that we are forgotten, and feel ashamed, lonely and desperate. But, just then we hear the Good Shepherd calling our name, think of it He knows our name, and we know His voice. He finds us, pats us, and puts us over

His shoulders and takes us back to where we belong.

JEHOVAH-SHAMMAH

The book of Ezekiel ends in a very unusual way by introducing to us Jehovah-*Shammah*-The LORD who is there! The context of Ezekiel is the challenge of building the city of Jerusalem. Even the name of this city connotes peace as it means the city of peace. But, God makes it clear the only way we can have peace is by knowing He is there. He is Jehovah- *Shammah*, the God who is there. And this city is to be a special city, because He is there.

When Jesus came into the world he came as Jehovah-*Shamma*, to make God present to us. His name was Immanuel which means "God with us" (Matt. 1:23). Jesus wants us to live in His presence. This is why when after his death and resurrection He would ascend into heaven so the Holy Spirit the comforter could come and be present in all of us who believe. Our bodies are now the Temples of God where God is Jehovah-*Shammah*, the God who is present in us (1 Corinthians 3:16).

JEHOVAH-TSIDKENU

Satan the Identity Thief will try to fill our lives with noise, confusion and needless activity so we lose sight of the presence of God. There is only one thing that can keep us from experiencing the presence of God that is sin, unrighteousness. And even when sin is crouching at our door, it is not as if God leaves us. We must understand the difference between relationship and fellowship. Sin can never cut off our relationship with God, but it is Satan's tool to disturb our fellowship with God. The old saying goes, "If you think God is far away, guess who moved." We moved, we wondered into some sin box, and God seems distant. During these times we desperately need to apply the truth about righteousness to our lives.

Satan will usually try to get us to approach righteousness from a religious standpoint. He will try to get us to work for it, sacrifice for it, or fake it till we make it and we never will. Righteousness can not be earned and it is not deserved, it is our free gift as a result of Jesus Christ's work and our faith, it is a free gift of grace.

In the Old Testament Jeremiah told us that righteousness was the key to salvation and sanctification. "In his days Judah will be saved and Israel will live in safety. This is the name by which He will be called: the LORD our righteousness" (Jeremiah 23:6). This is where we learn one of God's great Jehovah names: Jehovah-*Tsidkenu*, The LORD is our righteousness.

Isaiah made it clear that it is our sins, out unrighteousness that keeps us from God. But Isaiah also says, "surely the arm of the LORD is not too short to save, nor his ear to dull to hear" (Isaiah 59:1). In the Gospel, the good-news, Jesus preached we learn about Jehjovah-*Tsidkenu*. Paul made it clear, "for in the Gospel a righteousness from God is revealed a righteousness that is by faith, from first to last, just as it is written: the righteous will live by faith" (Romans 1:17).

Jesus himself is our righteousness; He is our Jehovah-*Tsidkenu*. And we are to rely on Him by faith. The Apostle Paul pulls all these great thoughts together in one power-packed passage in 1 Corinthians 1:30-31, he said, "It is because of Him that you are in Christ Jesus, who has become for us wisdom from God—that is our righteousness, holiness, and redemption. Therefore, as it is written, "let him who boasts boast in the Lord.""

There are three things we need to know about God.

#1. He is God.
#2. We are not Him
#3. Our lives become secure and purposeful as we
     get to know Him in His Jehovah names.

A regular study of these names will keep your heart thrilled and constantly remind us of who we are in Him. We find security from identity theft by the simple practice of regularly meditating on God's Jehovah names. We must make this our practice, and it is a wonderful way to pray and worship, try it. Just make each of His names a thank-you prayer to God.

- Jehovah-Jireh- The LORD my provider (Genesis 22:14)
- Jehovah-Rophe- The LORD my healer (Exodus 15:26)
- Jehovah-Nissi- The LORD my banner (Exodus 17:15)

- Jehovah-Mekeddeshem-The LORD who sanctifies me (Lev. 20:7-8)
- Jehovah-Shalom-The LORD is my peace (Judges 6:24)
- Jehovah-Rohi-The LORD is my shepherd (Psalm 23)
- Jehovah-Shammah-The LORD is present in me (Ezekiel. 48:35)
- Jehovah-Tsidkenu-The LORD is my righteousness (Jeremiah 23:6)
- Jehovah-Savior-The Lord Jesus is my savior!

Sid quip: If we have a small God we have big problems, if we have a big God we have small problems. The issue is always, how big is our God?

When we meditate on these great names we lose ourselves in God's greatness. This is why the Bible records God's Jehovah names, they impart identity and make us secure, "Like a Rock!"

Chapter 8
RESPECT OUR ROOT

Romans 11:18

Rodney Dangerfield, a famous American comic, said he didn't get "no respect". He said his parents gave him an electric toaster and an electric radio as bath toys, and then he said, "See, I told you I don't get no respect." And we remember him rolling his eyes and shaking his head as we laughed.

I was raised with respect being taught to me as an important virtue. Respect was imparted to me as an identity attribute, it was who we were. I was instructed to show respect to all human beings because we are made in the image of God; I was taught to walk old people across the street and to open doors for ladies. We men took our hats off in buildings, and I said, "yes sir" and "yes or no ma'm". And when I became a Christian, respect made even more sense to me because it is consistent with the life Jesus had given to me.

When any Gentile comes to Jesus, we don't just get a new life and identity in Him, we get grafted into His forever family, Israel. We therefore need to learn to show respect for this "Kingdom of Priests, and this Holy Nation", that we now belong in by grace (Romans 2).

There are many symbols that are used to help people identity with Israel. The Star of David, The Menorah, and the olive tree. Paul uses a horticultural illustration to explain our relationship to Israel and to help us understand our new identity and our place in the Jewish family. Yes, you heard it right. If you are a Christian, you are a Jew; your heart has been circumcised and you have been adopted into God's forever family (Ephesians 1:12, Romans 8:23, 9:4).

For us former Gentiles there are a lot of changes we need to understand. For one, we need to realize we are no longer Gentiles, for that is an immoral and unspiritual identity. There are only two people groups in the world at anytime, Jews (the people belonging to God). and Gentiles (people who do not belong to God.). We need to understand that it is by grace that we have been grafted in to Israel, and so we need to show grace to all people, Jew and Gentile. Grace to the Jew for including us, and grace to Gentiles so they will know that they can be included.

The Apostle Paul said, "Do not boast over those branches. If you do, consider this, 'you do not support the root, but the root supports you' (Romans 11:18)." This is our primary reason for learning to show respect, as it is by grace we have been grafted into the olive tree. We were once a stand alone wild branch and now we have been tied into the root by spiritual surgery. The "tree specialist," God the vine dresser (John 15), made a slit with a knife into the root stalk and placed us as a twig into that slit and we began to grow attached to the root. We have been held there on complete "life-support" ever since this miracle of grace took place. We owe everything to Israel. Israel's four pillars of faith, God, Torah (the first five books of the Old Testament), God's people and the Promised Land are the foundations of our faith. The Christian faith and the Jewish faith share the same Father God, the same fathers of the faith, the same Torah (the first five books of the Old Covenant), and the same Holy Spirit and Messiah.

Some Bible scholars make a strong case for the Root being the Patriarchs of Abraham, Isaac and Jacob. I don't know if we have to be so specific here, but Paul did say, "for I tell you that Christ has become a servant of the Jews on behalf of God's truth, to confirm the promises to the Patriarchs so that the Gentiles may glorify God for His mercy, as it is written, 'therefore I will praise you among the Gentiles; I will sing hymns to praise your name.'"

Satan is the Identity Thief, and throughout history he has constantly attacked the identity of the Jew. He has tried to make being a Gentile glamorous, and being a Jew reason enough to be exterminated. Anti-Semitism was a rallying call as Adolph Hitler fostered Jew hate, to call Germany to an Arian cause and the atrocities of World War Two. And, sadly, the church of Jesus did not have a strong enough understanding of their true identity as Jews to stand up to this holocaust. If Christian people today do not establish their identity in the root and respect the root, we will see another holocaust, or "Shoah", which means "catastrophe" and is often the preferred word to describe the attempted extermination of the Jews during WWII. There is a tremendous amount of Jew hate in the world today and sadly most western churches have remained passive and don't fully understand our true identity as Jews, and our relationship to the root.

As I see it, most evangelical churches are acting like they are "gentile-Christians", this is like saying they are "pagan Christians." Most act is if they are independent of Israel and yet proclaim they are identified with Jesus. When it comes to our identity we will see that we are either a Christian/Jew or we are aligned as a Gentile/pagan. There is no such thing as a Gentile-Christian, for when a person comes to Jesus they are grafted in to the Jewish olive tree, and are intrinsically identified with Israel. This is our true identity and our true DNA.

The words pagan and heathen mean "uncivilized" and "godless", and the word Gentile means any person who is not Jewish. Therefore it is wrong for a Christian person to see themselves as a Gentile, because they are now no longer without God, excluded from God, and on the outside in the heath. Being in Christ means that we have been brought near, and included in God's forever family. Our problem is our tendency for independence, and our dislike of identifying with some people we might not like. Someone once told me you can pick your friends, but you are stuck with your relatives. So just as a man or a woman who gets married, they don't just get a mate, they get in-laws. This can be seen from the negative, but choose to look at it from the positive.

From the positive, we are now in Abraham's family and he is really cool. God made some huge promises to Abraham like, "I will bless those who bless you and whoever curses you I will curse; and all the peoples of the earth will be blessed through you" (Genesis 12:3). And in Genesis 18:18, Abraham is told that he would be the father of a great and powerful nation. Abraham is also featured in the book of Romans as the example of faith. We are told that he was declared righteous because of his faith before he was circumcised. Paul uses this example to explain to us that we are accepted by God and brought into His family by faith alone. Just like Abraham was accepted by his faith, in other words, Abraham took God at His Word; God responded to this faith and declared Him righteous. The same is true with us who believe today. Paul concludes his letter to the Galatians by saying, "If you belong to Christ, then you are Abraham's seed, and heirs according to the promise" (Galatians 3:29).

Jesus is our ultimate example of cherishing Jewishness. Even though He came to His own people, and experienced great rejection, He always identified with Israel and never rejected the Jewish people. Jesus is our God, our Savior, our life, our identity and a marvelous Jewish example. He was born of Jewish parents and even was descended in the linage of David. He was circumcised on the eighth day according to the custom of the covenant. Jesus celebrated the Passover, the Festival of Lights/ Feast of Dedication (also known as Hanukkah). And as a little boy He would go with His parents to synagogue, and was known to teach God's precepts there. Jesus told us that He did not come to abolish the law, but rather fulfill it. He also said that He came to find the "lost sheep of Israel" (Matt. 5:24). The disciples He called to be with Him, were Jews, and He used Old Testament models to form His church. He approached His kingdom as a continuation of God's plans for Israel. Jesus always modeled respect for His Heavenly Father, The Law, the Patriarchs, the people of God and the Promised Land of Israel.

It is surprising to see a rough and rugged fisherman become a model of respect, but this is what happened to Peter. Peter showed his respect for the root in many ways. I am sure this brash fisherman had very "colorful" language, yet being with Jesus changed him and he said, "young men in the same way be submissive to those who are older than you, clothe yourselves with humility toward one another because, "God opposes the proud but gives grace to the humble." Humble yourselves, therefore under God's mighty hand, that He may lift you up in due time" (I Peter 5:5-6). And this is exactly Peter's life story; Jesus lifted Him up in many ways.

Peter was an unschooled and very ordinary man who became an extraordinary preacher (Acts 4:13). As he preached his many impromptu sermons he called upon many historically Jewish events and Jewish prophecy to proclaim Jesus as the Messiah. Peter began several of his sermons by saying "fellow Jews, or he would say, "Men of Israel", (Acts 2), then he would quote a prophet like Joel, or tell about King David, or quote Moses. And when he talked about God the Father he said, "The God of Abraham, Isaac, and Jacob, the God of our Fathers." Peter boldly used his Jewish roots to respectfully persuade people to believe in Jesus.

Peter would also write two Epistles, 1 & 2 Peter, that would inspire young converts to find their identity in Jesus and in Judaism. He had several solid themes firmly rooted in Judaism: salvation, the Word, Living Stones, submission, hope, humility, and the Day of the Lord. All of these are strong and famous Hebrew themes and Peter was an effective instrument to show us Jesus in these New Testament uses.

Peter is one of the most dramatic identity transformations in the Bible; he is what we call an "extreme makeover." In his early days with Jesus we see him being impulsive, inconsistent and absurd. But, he became what Jesus predicted and what Jesus saw in him, a rock. What Jesus sees in us can produce a dramatic transformation of our identity, too!

Peter speaks to our identity with several Jewish thoughts when he says the young believers, even Gentile converts, who read his letters, "But you are a chosen people, a Royal Priesthood, a Holy Nation, a people belonging to God, that you may declare the praises of Him who called you out of darkness into His wonderful light. Once you were not a people but now you are the people of God" (1 Peter 2:9-10). I think he is saying, once we didn't have a good identity, but now in Jesus we are chosen, royal, holy and we have the identity as Jews, because we now are God's children.

Many western American independent preachers who identity themselves as Gentiles are making a serious mistake when they say that the Apostle Paul, the Apostle to the Gentiles, quit seeing himself as a Jew. Certainly Paul stressed the believer's identity being found in Jesus, but he never renounced or denied his Jewish origin. He even went on to say that he would rather die than see his countrymen remain lost and without God (Romans 9:1-4). But, to consider yourself as a Gentile is to see yourself as a pagan, and as an idolater. I am curious as to what Paul would say to today's Post-moderns who are so Greek in that they emphasize feelings and experiences as being more important that truth. It seems to me that the church today has a choice to make, are we going to move toward Mars Hill and a Greek/Gentile identity? Or are we going to return to Mt. Sinai where Moses came down with the Law and embrace the precious boundary Mt. Truth can provide us with? I am not saying we should become legalistic, or come under the laws again, but I am saying we desperately need to respect God's Word again, both the Old and the New Testaments (Covenants).

The Apostle Paul, who so strongly emphasized the grace of God and personal faith in God, explained to us that the stronger we become in our biblical faith the more Jewish we would be and we would be more respectful of our Jewish heritage. Paul in Romans 2:29 explains how the believer experiences "heart circumcision" and becomes a true Jew as the Holy Spirit gives the believer a new heart. He also stresses the Jewishness of the Christian movement by reminding us that the Jews were entrusted with the Word of God, faith and righteousness (Romans 3:2-5).

This young, struggling first century church had to wrestle with its identity from the start. Paul clearly articulated that a Gentile who believes has passed from death and into life, and has gone from being without God to having a relationship with God and thus they are now a Jew. But, does this truth now mean that the new convert must be circumcised like a boy who grew up in a Hebrew family, with their laws and rituals?

Paul addressed the Jerusalem council (Acts 15) and helped insure the inclusion of these former Gentiles into this new sect of Judaism (the church), who are now, in reality, Christian Jews. Paul did this by persuading this council to see that salvation is by grace alone, and that the Holy Spirit had been miraculously transforming these Gentiles who were placing their faith in Jesus and repenting of their sins. It took an emphasis on respect from both sides of this issue to see their way clear, and make these new converts feel like they belonged in the olive tree.

Paul stressed time and time again that there is only one God, One faith, one Baptism, One Lord and Savior, one way of salvation, and that there is only one New Covenant in the Blood of Christ. He would strongly attack the modern preachers who preach a "dual covenant" that says there is a covenant for Jews and there is a covenant for Christians. He would call this discrimination and a severe form of persecution that would prevent Jews today from coming to Jesus. How can they hear without a preacher, and if they don't go and preach, how can they hear? (Romans 10). Paul was passionate about the gospel, about righteousness by faith alone and preaching about this marvelous grace. It was a happy day for him, when the former Gentiles were not encumbered by the laws and rituals, but we need to cherish the inclusion in the olive tree.

Respect is the key if life in the olive tree is to be peaceful. Using this tree image, it is absurd to think of one branch in a tree sparing with another branch; a tree shouldn't have a bickering problem. Regardless, Paul makes a plea for honor, humility and respect when he uses the word "remember" in this Ephesians 2 passage. He said, "Therefore, remember that formerly you, who are Gentiles by birth and called "uncircumcised" by those who call themselves "the circumcision", remember that at that time you were separate from Christ, excluded from citizenship in Israel and foreigners to the covenants of the promise, without hope, and without God in the world. But now in Christ Jesus you who once were far away have been brought near through the blood of Christ. For He himself is our peace, who has made the two one" (Eph. 2:11-12).

Jesus modeled this humility and Peter and Paul are marvelous examples of honor and humility. Both Peter and Paul went from being brash and arrogant to becoming grateful and humble servants who lived to honor Jesus. Both of these men had their arrogance and pride crucified when they trusted Jesus, and appeal to all of us in the same olive tree, to be humble and peaceful for the glory of God and for the unity of the Spirit. In Romans 11 Paul told us that it is the root that supports the branches, and every former Gentile has a reason to be humble, because we are on "life-support" from the root.

Therefore Paul exhorts us to, "be completely humble and gentle; be patient, bearing with one another in love, Make every effort to keep the unity of the Spirit through the bond of peace" (Ephesians 4:2). And in Colossians 3 he tells us to "rid yourselves of all such things as these; anger, rage, malice, slander, and filthy language from your lips. Do not lie to each other, since you have taken off your old self with its practices and have put on the new self which is being renewed in the image of its Creator. Here there is no Greek or Jew, circumcised or uncircumcised, barbarian, Scythian slave or free, but Christ is all and is in all. Therefore, as God's chosen people, holy and dearly loved, clothe yourselves with compassion, kindness, humility, gentleness, and patience. Bear with each other and forgive whatever grievances you may have against one another. Forgive as the Lord forgave you. And over all these virtues put on love, which binds them together in perfect unity" (Col. 3:8-13).

This exhortation from Paul is so similar to the prayer Jesus prayed for us in the Garden of Gethsemane the night before His crucifixion where he made the way possible for ex-Gentiles and Jews to live out of the same olive tree. Incidentally, the name Gethsemane means olive press. This is where Jesus so intently prayed for us to believe and then He focused His prayer on the unity in this olive tree. His prayer was so intense that His sweat was like drops of blood (John 17).

Respect for the root is the needed response from all of us who find our life and identity in the olive tree. As former Gentiles we need to be very humble because it is only by the grace and mercy of God that we have been grafted in. There is nothing for us to boast in except for this grace, as the root supports us completely. We don't do anything but abide and draw our life from the root. But, do we really know what respect is? We are living in a culture that now only rarely stops to let a funeral procession pass by.

I think the way to show our high regard, high esteem, appreciation, and gratitude for being grafted into this olive tree is best done by learning to let the SAP flow. I say it this way: the Spirit and the Anointing are released by Praise. As all of us in the olive tree lift our heads, arms, hands and hearts to God in praise because he causes the SAP of his Holy Spirit to flow through us. I call this spiritual "photosynthesis", and just as a tree lifts its branches and exposes its leaves to the sun above, the miracle of "fruit" begins to form. The branch never produces fruit, as all it can do is bear it. This same truth applies to us who live to praise God.

To let the SAP flow I have developed an acrostic from the word respect that will help position our hearts so the SAP can flow.

R- Reverence for God
E- Encourage faith
S- Spirit (walk in the Spirit)
P- Pray (focus on prayers of thanksgiving and praise)
E- Edification (focus on building others up)
C- Character (the fruit of the Spirit are the character qualities of Jesus Gal.5:22-23)
T- Truth: live it, love it and rely upon it.

This is an acrostic that will help us learn to respect our root. But, there are some practical things we can do to show respect for the root.

1. Learn that Old Testament! (Get to know the great old stories, the Laws, the feasts and festivals, and see how the prophecies are fulfilled in Jesus)
2. Honestly assess your life; are you doing any thing to allow a dejudiazation to happen in your life, your family, your church or your community?
3. Do not allow any Gentile, or pagan thinking or behavior to flow out of your life as this is inconsistent with your true identity in the root
4. Bear fruit that brings glory to God (Gal. 5:22-23)[9]
5. Confront the heresy of dual covenant and replacement theology whenever you see it (one covenant for Jews and another for Gentiles)
6. Encourage your church to practice its Jewishness and encourage your Pastor to teach on the Old Testament people, places, prophecy and practices (Encourage your Pastor to include the Menorah and the study of the Feast of Dedication in your Christmas experience. And

---

[9] See Appendix #1, p. 219, Pyramid to Victory.

during Easter time, study the Passover and consider celebrating a Seder)
7. Let the SAP flow in your own life, by abiding in the vine, and giving praise to God for grafting you into his precious olive tree.

The olive tree is a life-giving tree. Please take the time to meditate on the many identity issues contained in this tree. Prayerfully consider God's heart and picture your role in the tree. As we do this we will experience a glorious unity. We must all humble our hearts and respect God, His people, and His plan. When we do this we will foil the Identity Thief and help ourselves and people everywhere find security from identity theft.

Chapter 9
OWN YOUR OWN GOOD NAME

Proverbs 22:1

I loved recess. I should say that when I was in grade school I lived for recess. I would daydream about playing tag, riding the teeter totter, hanging on the monkey bars, and practicing track and field events. The country school I attended had a recess time where the whole school went to the playground together for recess. Let me tell you, when you are a skinny little fourth grader and the seventh graders are out there, you feel like a little gerbil among the gorillas.

While waiting my turn on the monkey bars, I noticed and overheard a circle of seventh grade boys talking. One of the taller boys was pointing at me while he talked, and I heard him say, "That boy's grandpa killed my brother." I immediately hung my head and was emotionally paralyzed because I knew what he said was true. My grandpa had accidentally run into his brother while driving home from work. I'll never forget that day. Within an hour after the accident Grandpa was in our driveway talking about this tragedy with my parents. I overheard some of the gruesome details, but what I will always remember was Grandpa's solemn tone and his pale, ashen complexion; he was truly sorry.

During this moment on the playground there was a quantum skip of time in my mind. I think I stood there motionless trying to get my fourth grade brain to comprehend the pain, and the connection of my grandpa to me. Why was I being singled out for something my grandpa did? And how was I to respond? Why should I have a bad name because my grandpa was involved in a tragic accident? I know there is guilt by association, but I wasn't going to love my grandpa less. I knew he needed me to love him more. Nothing he did could change the fact that he drove his car into this boy. I am sure this was purely unintentional. I know Grandpa wanted to move from the neighborhood, but he faced up to his wrong and did all he could to comfort this family. Can you imagine standing before this Mom and Dad and telling them about your responsibility for such an accident?

Until this accident all I knew was that my family had a good name in our community. Everywhere I went I heard good things about my dad, my aunt and uncle, and especially Grandma's cooking. It seemed as if doors opened up for me because of my family's good name. Our family has had a real estate business in our town for nearly a hundred and twenty years, and you just don't do business for that long in the same place without a good name. But, back in the fourth grade, I had to reckon with a different reality; in the minds of these boys I had a bad name. Would they try to rough me up? Play pranks on me? They did none of it, but I did have a few dark nights in my soul thinking about my identity, and cursing this fatal accident Grandpa was responsible for.

When thousands upon thousands of immigrants came to America, all of these people were challenged to blaze a new life, but every one of them had a decision to make about their name. I think it would be very interesting to see the changes that took place at those desks on Ellis Island as these people signed in and registered their name. To some it was humbling to realize that none of their family history would roll over and benefit them here in the new land. To others, I bet they changed their name to distance themselves from some bad reputations. Wouldn't it be nice to get rid of a gangster reputation or a drunkard's legacy? What if your family was known for its house of ill repute? And what if your family had a reputation for bad craftsmanship? Get rid of it with a new name!

If I had a last name like Pol Pot, Mussolini, Stalin, or Hitler, I'd do everything I could to change my name, because with names like these your first impression would always be negative. Surprise, surprise, surprise, I looked in my local phone book and none of these names are listed. I had a step grandmother who talked like she was related to all the "good families" in America. She called herself a "blueblood"; she meant she thought she had a good pedigree. This "blue blood" label is an English expression about a noble birth. It means being pure or free from Moorish or Jewish blood. Her attitude made me nauseous; I wish I had Jewish blood flowing in my body. Who was she to say that her genes were better? It was difficult to hold a civil conversation with this woman because her pride in her pedigree always oozed out. And when it came out it had a serious stink to it, because she always wanted me to know that her name was better than mine. I always wanted to tell her that her name was mud until she married my grandfather. Their relationship with each other was adulterous, and I believe she was trying to mask her guilt and shame with this "blue blood" talk.

When I was in high school I remember observing my friend and teammate try to give himself a cool nickname. It was like he had to entice and bribe his friends to use it. I thought, "who gets to name himself?" When my sister was born her given name was Mary, but since I couldn't enunciate "r", her name came out Mimi and she has been Mimi ever since. You and I can't pick our names, not even our nicknames, and if our family was once a bunch of axe murderers, or "blue-bloods", it is only fodder for the Identity Thief to use to distort our identity; neither shame or pride has to be the tag of a Child of God.

Can you imagine a new born baby laying in her hospital crib and protesting the name that is being placed on her crib and wristband? Imagine this baby girl throwing a tantrum and shouting, "I don't like the name Teresa! I shall be called Tammy!" Silly, you say, and I agree. There are lots of things we don't get to choose in this life, like our parents, where we are born, our sex, our talents, our personality, and we don't get to choose our name. Or do we?

When a person believes in Jesus and is born again by the Spirit of God, that person gets a new nature, a new character, a new destiny, and a new identity. God gives that new born person His divine name. This name is packed with blessing and esteem. Solomon wrote, "A good name is more desirable than great riches; to be esteemed is better than silver or gold" (Proverbs 22:1). This is the good name the Identity Thief can't touch, and it is the believers address, access, business and success.

As a child growing up, I always wanted to go out to eat. We children would always gang up on dad and bargain and whine to try to get him to take us out to dinner. Dad always stayed resolute and always answered we will go out to eat at "twenty-o-eight." This was his way of saying we are going to eat another boring meal at home (our home address was "twenty-o-eight)." Then he would brag on the great meals Mom made for us, and tell us about the starving children in Africa. If you have ever read about heaven in the Bible, there is a lot of good eating going on there. It is a wedding party, and a banquet table. Even more important than eating, heaven is our new address and it is a prestigious address. Imagine your next set of envelopes with this address printed as the return address? Think of it, where we are living now is only a temporary dwelling place.

Peter, a disciple of Jesus, was once just a bumbling fisherman until he stumbled on this truth. He said it this way, "Praise be to the God and Father of our Lord Jesus Christ! In His great mercy He has given us new birth into a living hope through the resurrection of Jesus Christ from the dead, into an inheritance that can never perish, spoil or fade—kept in heaven for you, who through faith and shielded by God's power until the coming of the salvation that is ready to be revealed in the last time" (1 Peter 1:3-5).

When Peter was introduced to Jesus by his brother Andrew, Peter's identity and eternal address changed. Before Jesus came into his life his address was, "big dumb fisherman, Sea of Galilee, look for the boat with the messed up nets." Now he has a new address, "Simon Peter, a servant and apostle of Jesus Christ, to those who through the righteousness of our God and Savior Jesus Christ have received a faith as precious as ours; Grace and peace be yours in abundance through the knowledge of God and Jesus our Lord" (2 Peter 1:1-2). Now that is a prestigious new identity and address!

Peter knew everything about his life had changed when he met Jesus, even his address. His mail box was now placed in heaven. Peter once objected to Jesus going to the cross to die, and then to ascend into heaven to "prepare a place" for him. Peter didn't always understand what Jesus had to do, but now that Jesus had died for all his sins, and was raised from the dead by the Holy Spirit, I am sure Peter would like the King James version of this text because it goes this way, "In my Father's house are many mansions" (John 14:2). God has given us this prestigious address and it as with it benefits for the here and the hereafter.

While attending seminary, Karen and I lived on millionaire row. We lived as caretakers for some very wealthy people to be exact;

we lived one house down the street from a billionaire. And when people asked us where we lived we often had instant clout if they knew our street. Think about it, we were given immediate respect because we had a prestigious address. Consider your address in heaven: our street is paved with pure gold (Revelation 21:21), and it is a "gated" community!

Our future address is an identity power assist for us in the here and now! This reality can make a difference in our everyday lives. While most people toil all their days to get a home with a good address, we already have one. And while most people covet gold and rightly so (at six hundred and fifty dollars an ounce I see why), but when the invoice is tallied today's gold is just road base. Now that thought will put our lives into a better and more uplifting perspective.

Our name is good not because we were so good or because of the legacy of our parents and grand parents, we have a good name in spite of what ever has gone before us, because Jesus has adopted us into His forever family! We have His name and address. The Apostle Paul said, "He predestined us to be adopted as sons through Jesus Christ." And now we have His name, His full inheritance, His address, and full rights as sons. All because of God's grace toward us expressed in Jesus sacrificial death for our sins and assured by our faith in Him. All of this is based on the reliability of God's Holy Word, and His promises are true (Galatians 4:5-6, 2 Corinthians 1:20).

We should take a minute and think about the name that gives us our identity and permanent address. Paul said about Jesus, "Therefore God exalted him to the highest place and gave him the name that is above every name, that at the name of Jesus every knee should bow, in heaven and on earth and under the earth, and every tongue confess that Jesus Christ is Lord to the glory of God the Father" (Philippians 2:9-11). Our new checks have this great name on them and best of all He has already paid the bill (Phil 4:19).

It is amazing how this address and this name gives us access to the best of everything. Names like Rockefeller, Kennedy, Hunt, Gates, Buffett, or Ford always get special privileges. I think we would all be amazed at all the sweet deals these folks get because of the prestige of their name. Shoot fire, Paris Hilton gets paid to party at high falootin' places. Years ago I worked for some fine folks who owned a five-star rated guest ranch. The owner told me that once one of these families that boast of one of these names attended their ranch, and when it was time to pay the bill they said they didn't have to because of their name. Well this owner had to press this issue all the way back to Washington, and I will give you a hint as to what family this was: a long time ago they bootlegged alcohol and this is how they acquired their first bit of wealth. Needless to say, no wonder they stay rich, they don't think they have to pay; I'd be rich too if I didn't pay, but I would only be rich in this world's way. Think about it, if your name is Joe Shmo and you present your business plan to a corporation, often your plan is thrown into the trash. But, if you have a prestigious name, your plan goes right to the top of the pile and maybe straight into the board room.

When Jesus launched His kingdom ministry he quoted Isaiah 61, "the Spirit of the sovereign LORD is on me, because the LORD has anointed me to preach good news to the poor. He has sent me to bind up the broken hearted, to proclaim freedom for the captives and release from darkness for the prisoners, to proclaim the year of the LORD'S favor and the day of vengeance of our God. To comfort all who mourn, and provide for those who grieve in Zion—to bestow on them a crown of beauty instead of ashes, the oil of gladness instead of mourning, and a garment of praise instead of a spirit of despair, they will be called oaks of righteousness a planting of the LORD for the display of His splendor" (Isaiah 61:1-3).

Jesus is telling us that He is leveling the playing field, in the grand scheme of things the people with the worldly clout just might not measure up if they are relying on this world's status for their identity. Here we see Him giving his followers significance and confidence. If we are not careful we can allow the Identity Thief to overwhelm us with thoughts of inadequacy, despair, and a spirit of heaviness. These attitudes cause us to get stuck in the mud of doubt and feeling like we are hapless and hopeless creatures who don't deserve the oxygen we are breathing. It is easy to start thinking that we are not going to get any breaks, we mumble about not having the name, the looks, the money, or the connections. But, Jesus will encourage us if we choose to win the battle of believing, and the Identity Thief can be stiff armed with just a word, and that word is the name Jesus.

As we learn to listen to God we begin to hear Him speak encouragement to our human spirit; he lifts us up. Remember Peter? He is the guy we always see splashing around like he is drowning and the Lord lifts Him up. Peter had moments of despair but he is the one who would write, "Humble yourselves, therefore, under God's mighty hand, that he may lift you up in due time. Cast all your anxiety on him because he cares for you" (1 Peter 5:6-7). Because we bear his name, and own his good name as our own, he promises us that we have access to his throne of grace. In Isaiah 61 he told us that he will lift our broken hearts, release us from being stuck, reward our grief with the crown of beauty, and exchange our mourning for gladness. The key to this awesome access is to believe for it, and to thank and praise God for it. The Bible says we enter His courts with thanksgiving and praise. David said, "Enter his gates with thanksgiving and his courts with praise; give thanks to him and praise his name" (Psalm 100:4).

I call it letting the SAP flow; I believe the Spirit and the Anointing are released by Praise.[10] To be a bit technical, I call it Spiritual Photosynthesis!" This miracle of God happens every moment in nature as the trees lift their branches to the sunshine above. Energy is absorbed in the leaves of the needles and signals the roots to soak up the moisture and release the sap throughout the tree. The sap flows and we see little buds, then flowers and soon we see the fruit, and it is as if the tree is doing nothing but being a tree. In a spiritual way we are to be a tree, and lift our hearts to God, access the throne of grace in praise and thanksgiving and simply by abiding in Christ through faith in Him the Holy Spirit causes the SAP to flow, the Spirit and the Anointing are released throughout our being and into our relationships (to learn more, meditate on John chapter 15). As we abide in Jesus who is the vine, before long we are abounding in SAP and we are transformed naturally, we go from little often trampled saplings into "oaks of righteousness, who display the splendor of the LORD (Isaiah 61:3).

---

[10] See Appendix #1, p.219, Pyramid to Victory.

Access to the throne of grace is granted us because of our good name, which is really the name of Jesus (Hebrews 4:16). When we own our good name we can afford to be a little nuts and outlandishly bold, because giant oak trees were once just little nuts that held their ground. In other words, be a little nut who owns your good name!

Our direct access to God in prayer means that we have special resources available to us at all times. The scriptures declare that wisdom is always available (James 1:5): counsel, comfort, peace and favor are in ready supply. Therefore we don't need to pout and act like we never get the breaks. We just need to learn to appropriate our access to God and believe that He is accepted in more places than American Express®.

Our good name is not only our address and our access, this is our primary business. We hear a lot of talk in business about "branding". Corporations are learning to pay attention to their identity in the marketplace. I remember twenty years ago the environmentalists were regularly attacking the Weyerhaeuser Corporation for the way they would strip a mountainside of timber with their practice of clear cutting. Today, Wayerhaeuser positions itself in the marketplace as the "tree growing company." Young people today probably don't have a clue as to what products this massive corporation sells but they have heard the positive spin by watching their well produced television ads. We will never see a chainsaw or a barren landscape in one of their commercials, but we will see foresters wearing a Wayerhaeuser logo shirt planting seedlings by the hundreds. This corporation is smart and they have learned that protecting their good name is their primary business.

Every good business in America works diligently to acquire and protect their good name because their business depends on it. I don't think we will ever see a company named "Enron" reenter the marketplace. Their poor leadership, bad financial practices and blatant greed has botched that name forever. Firestone had image problems years ago because they had a tire that failed to support the Ford Explorer SUV. Both of these American companies had to work hard to change the public perception of their products and their respective company. Recently Ford Motor Company has nudged up to Toyota in customer satisfaction and quality. This is a quantum leap and a sign that they are winning on two fronts, the business of a positive identity, and putting out a great product.

Have you ever taken some time to consider how the Identity Thief seeks to destroy your identity and your reputation? I have found that he relishes the opportunity to exploit any hypocrisy. Any lie, any poor performance, and any form of adultery will be constantly replayed. Just look at the tabloids and how they attack any person who had identified with Jesus. Mel Gibson is a prime example. He has never claimed perfection, yet when he had a few drinks too many and let his tongue wag too much in an angry barrage, he was crucified in the media. The best thing we can do to own our good name is to understand what King David said in the famous Twenty third Psalm.

David said, "He makes me lie down in green pastures, He leads me beside quiet waters, He restores my soul. He guides me in the paths of righteousness for His name's sake." What he is saying is that like sheep we need to take some time out and allow ourselves to be settled down. As a shepherd David said he had to make the sheep lie down, and this is the truth. We get so worked up and fueled by adrenaline that left to ourselves we would be like the Energizer Bunny and just keep going and going. We would be going in the direction of trouble and like the old adage says, "the hurriedier I go, the behinder I get." It is when we live the hurried life is when we make the poor decisions that prevent us from living out of our good name. In the hurriedness we forget that we are living for "his namesake."

We must accept our responsibility to slow down, lie down, relax and smell the flowers, drink in the good water, and breathe the fresh air. In this context the shepherd is able to protect his sheep from predators, and in our case Jesus our good shepherd is able to protect us from the Identity Thief. After some rest the shepherd will then go around from sheep to sheep and prop them up with his staff, message their legs because they went numb while lying on their backs and their wool coats would be heavy with dew in the grass. This is what David meant when he says he restores their souls. In the same way when we rest in the Lord, He restores our lives so we are ready and willing to walk in the paths of righteousness for His name sake.

This path is not a path to nowhere, and it is not the wide road that leads to destruction, it is the narrow road that leads to life (Matthew 7:13). The Bible makes it clear that when we follow the shepherd we don't just walk wherever our feet take us, we are to walk in His footsteps (1 Peter 2:21). This is why it is so important for us to study the life of Jesus in the New Testament. We need to learn not just what He said, but we need to observe what He did and how He did it. We need to own His name and walk in this world like He did. He didn't walk in the paths that lead to sin, he always took the highway of holiness. Remember that not even His enemies could accuse Him of sinning, because He always owned His good name.

When a person close to me was a freshman at the University in Lincoln Nebraska, some of my friends ran into him at a party after a football game there. I went to school in Kearney, but many of my friends would drive into Lincoln for the football games and the parties. On a Monday following one of these weekends my friends told me how they had seen my relative and that he had had too much alcohol to drink. I wrote him a letter and reminded him of how we shared the same family name and strongly encouraged him to own his good name. At the time he did not know the Lord Jesus so he didn't believe the same way I did about finding our identity in the good name of Jesus. I remember feeling quite compelled to drive to Lincoln and knock some sense into his skull, but I never did.

Today, I am grateful that he has come to find his life and identity in the Lord Jesus Christ. He is a life-giving Christian man, devoted husband, and the dad most kids wish they had. God did this miracle in his life and today he owns his own good name, which he knows is not his last name, or his first name, it is the name he has received by placing his faith in Jesus Christ, and by grace he now owns his own good name.

Today when I talk with people who believe in Jesus who are not walking in the paths of righteousness for His name sake, I don't threaten to knock some sense into their skulls, I simply remind them who they are. I say, "You know who you are, you wear the CROWN." This is my way of reminding people, be it my children or my friends, it is a way to encourage people to know that it is our primary business to represent Jesus by the way that we live, so walk in a manner worthy of Him (Phillipeans 1:27).

If you were a descendant of outlaw Jesse James or assassin John Wilkes Booth, or of a slave trader, a purveyor of pornography like Hugh Hefner, or an alcoholic, or a drug pusher, a womanizer or a child molester, I have good news for you. If your family name has been disgraced by you or someone else, by grace you can have the best name of all by believing in Jesus Christ. And He promises to help you to own this good name through the promises of his Word and the enablement of the Holy Spirit. Please do not let the Identity Thief get you to think you have a bad name, you don't have a bad name if you truly believe in Jesus. Enjoy the benefits that come with owning your good name (Psalm 103:1-4). When we take the name of Jesus and "name-it," that is claim his name as our own, this is when our identity begins to be established on the rock. By owning our good name, we become "like a rock" and have security from identity theft.

Wear the CROWN

Section Three:
ENGRAVE IT!

You yourselves are our letter, written on our hearts, known and read by everybody. You show that you are a letter from Christ, the result of our ministry, written not with ink but with the Spirit of the living God, not on tablets of stone but on the tablets of human hearts. Such confidence is ours through Christ before God. Not that we are competent in ourselves to claim anything for ourselves, but our competence comes from God.
2 Corinthians 3:2-5

For you died, and your life is now hidden with Christ in God. When Christ, who is your life appears, then you also will appear with him in glory.
Colossians 3:3

The word from the physical world we will use to describe what it means to have our true identity engraved on our hearts is the word **encryption**.

Encryption is an attempt to ensure secrecy in communications. Cryptography uses both mathematics and computer science to encrypt or convert ordinary information into unintelligible gibberish, so that the information or this identity can only be deciphered by those who are authorized. A cipher is a pair of algorithms which perform this encryption and the reversing decryption. Cryptography is used to provide security of our ATM cards, computer passwords and electronic passwords.

 World War II provides us with an interesting story

about encryption. Both the German military machine and the Japanese sent their military leaders secret information over the air waves in telegraph and radio transmissions. To do this they encrypted these messages in code. On the receiving end of these communications was an "Enigma Machine" that would decipher the code and deliver the official message. The allies (the Brits and the US forces) made great and valiant attempts to capture these machines and did so late in the war. Many believe that our great victory at sea, the Battle of Midway, was only possible because we had captured an Enigma Machine and were able to listen in on their orders.

The US military employed a very ingenious way of encrypting vital and top secret information. We implemented the language of the Navaho Indians who had a language that had never been recorded. To make this work, these great heroes, the Navahos, would both transmit the message and receive and communicate the message. If you want to see a great movie starring Nicholas Cage and these great American heroes, check out WIND TALKERS.

Something to think about: How does God use our trials and tribulations to engrave His code into our lives? (James 1:2-3, Romans 5:3-5)

Chapter 10
BADGES, LANYARDS, UNIFORMS, AND TRAMP STAMPS

Matthew 20:26-28, John 13:34-35

I met J.D. "Buck" Savage through a law enforcement friend of mine. This guy had an ego the size of Paul Bunyon, and he had a way of walking and talking that said "I am big and I am important." Buck is a character. He is not a real character even though some of his manner is way too life-like, he is a made up comedy personality that was created by Dave Smith. Dave is an internationally known motivational speaker and law enforcement trainer who takes "Buck" with him to train police officers. More often than not Dave puts old "Buck Savage" in situations where crime fighters can learn through Buck's bad example and learn what not to do when working with the public.

You see, "Buck" finds his identity in his bright and shiny police badge. As soon as Buck flashes his badge his testosterone level raises, his chest sticks out, and his gun begins to wag. If a man's identity is based on the number of items attached to his belt, then Buck is a man's man. He has black leather cases to hold a knife, hand-cuffs, a stick, a flash light, his chrome plated gun, and a neat line of bullets. But, what sets Buck apart from the rest of the world and the symbol of his worth is his badge. The day that badge was pinned to his chest was the best day of Buck's life. He acts like he believes he became a valuable person when that badge was fastened to his police shirt. His life is in his badge. He knows this to be true, and he loves how his badge wearing presence can instantly change the demeanor of any room.

I laughed my self silly watching one of these training videos where Buck showed us how to handle our gun in a public situation. In one scene old Buck comes sauntering into a local diner like Wyatt Earp braced for a show down. He has his police-issue tear drop sun glasses on just so, and his moustache is groomed to perfection. His hands are positioned near his belt, and Buck tells you to "watch the hands" (that's his line). As he makes his way to the counter he is as imposing as he can be, and then he pulls out his gun. The whole restaurant gasps and ducks under tables only to see Buck place that foreboding piece of steel on the counter. Everyone in the place is uncomfortable, but Buck smiles as if he is doing his job. He loves knowing that because of his badge, "the Buck stops here." He has started to believe that his identity is in his badge. We can only imagine how this would affect his home life and his friendships. But, like the rest of the restaurant, we breathe a sigh of relief when we realize this is just Dave Smith doing some play acting on how not to act as a law enforcement person.

Dave Smith very effectively uses this dramatic presentation to instruct law enforcement officers how to behave in public by showing them how not to handle their gun in a public situation. He uses humor to get law enforcement officers to look at "Buck" and see if by chance they have some Buck Savage "look at me, see my badge and fear my gun" attitudes in them. We have all witnessed people who have found their identity in the badge. When people hide behind their badge they are transformed from being a public servant to a power broker. It is easy to see how a police badge can make a person feel important. There are laws that protect the badge, and authority granted by our constitution, our country, the city where we live, and our courts back up the badge. But, the person who wears the badge needs to remember that they are not that authority, they represent the powers that be, but in of themselves they are a human being who has been asked to be a public servant.

Some law enforcement officers have been known to acquire what I call a "staff-infection." This is a disease that a law enforcement officer can pick up by touching the badge, wearing the uniform, and toting the gun. It is capable of changing the way a person thinks about him self or her self. There are people who go to the police academy with hopes of acquiring the badge and the position to get the feeling of significance. The Identity Thief has some strategies for influencing people who wear the badge. He will either try to get them to think that they are more important than they are and abandon the attitude of a public servant. He will try to corrupt those he can because of their position of influence. He will play to their power and convince them that they deserve to take a bribe because they are worth more than they are being paid. Or, he will get these servants so disillusioned about their insignificance that he will get them to disrespect what their badge represents, and influence sloppy police work.

The Identity Thief gets law enforcers to miss use their badge by controlling people and not serving the people. Now I know there are times when force is necessary and it is in these times a badge wearing officer needs to be extremely confident in their identity so that they can act out of a solid servant identity and do the right thing with dispatch. But, we all need to be careful not to do things to become somebody. We don't want our law enforcement people always trying to be the hero in a quest to become valued. We want law enforcement people to know that they are respected and valued because they have responded to the call, and have been trained to serve in this way. Jesus spoke about the proper attitude when he said, "whoever wants to become great among you must be your servant, and whoever wants to be first must be your slave" (Matthew 20:26-28).

Jesus made it clear the mark of a servant is not a badge, but it is a heart attitude that desires to show true care. I have used the word CARE as an acrostic to capture the meaning of whole hearted care. C-is for character, which is the commitment to do the right thing in the right way at the right time. A-is for attitude, the best attitude is always the humble and thankful attitude of a servant. R-is for respect, we want and need for people on both sides of the law or any situation to be respectfully treated because all involved are made in the image of God. And E- is for effort. Giving a whole hearted effort really does matter, because it truly shows that we care. If a person is called to be a public servant and they model this CARE principle, then these are the ones who can wear the badge, and handle the authority placed on them with grace.

Just as a badge can impute a sense of significance, so people try to find significance by wearing unusual strings. I heard a story about a string that didn't get any respect. This string came walking into a bar acting like a respectful string but as soon as the bartender saw this string he said, "We don't serve strings". And then he showed this string the door. The string went outside feeling discriminated against and downright disgusted. So worked up was this string that he began to twist and shout and shake himself until he became frayed. He then gathered himself up, straightened himself out by tying a knot in his loose ends and then mustered the courage to reenter the bar and ask the bartender for a drink. Just as soon as the door closed behind him, he heard the bartender yell out, "I told you we don't serve strings". This witty old string responded, "I'm a frayed-Knot". The bar tender was instantly tongue tied and had no response but to pour this string a drink.

The reason I tell this really dumb story about the string is to get your attention to realize that there are strings walking into establishments all over our town, and they don't feel like they get any respect. The string can make people feel like they are Rodney Dangerfield, the comedian of yesteryear who didn't get any respect. He said, "Last week I told my psychiatrist, 'I keep thinking about suicide.' He said from now on I have to pay in advance." Another time he said, "When I was a kid I got no respect. One time I was kidnapped, and the kidnappers sent my parents a note. They said we want five thousand dollars or you will see your kid again." Rodney rolled his big round eyes and said, "I tell you, with my doctor I don't get no respect. I told him, 'I've swallowed a bottle of sleeping pills.' He told me to have a few drinks and get some rest."

The string around a person's neck can make them feel like they don't get "no respect". Have you ever noticed the people in your community who have strings around their necks? These strings can be of various colors, but the thing about these strings is what they communicate to the wearer and the observer. These strings often have a plastic pouch attached to them, or a card with a magnetic strip or a bar code. For sure this string carries with it identity information and the wearer is tagged by this string. For some this string means significance, and for others this string means what Rodney Dangerfield used to say, "See, I don't get no respect!"

These strings are also called lanyards; we know them as cords worn around the neck or the wrist to carry something. This word has an old origin as it was once called a Dragoon. French soldiers would secure their saber to their wrist with one, so they could fire their pistol with their other hand. Calvary soldiers also began using this sword knot called a lanyard and determined this word to mean, "to force into submission." And now we see corporate America putting these lanyards around the necks of their employees and some of these wearers do feel like they are being forced into submission.

To some string wearing employees this lanyard means security, a pension plan, a parking space, and a desk with a chair to park their rear end. These people adore the employee handbook and thoroughly enjoy climbing the corporate ladder because their eyes are on the benefits of the stock options, dividends, insurance and the retirement plan. They think we get all of this for wearing a string, and conclude I will be mercenary because this with this string attached to my neck I am somebody. And there in lies the problem with strings, so many in corporate America have sold their soul to the corporation and they think the string means significance.

To others the string around their neck is just like a noose and they live in fear of the floor boards being dropped and there they are being hung by the string. They see the string as a ball and chain around their leg, and they are in bondage to the string. They know they have to give up their own personality to fit in to the corporation, so the string means fake it and never really make it. They know the string means they have to give up their own dreams because to be a corporate player there can't be any individuality. Shoot fire, they even have to change their language and acquire corporate speak, and their wardrobe must conform to the dress code as stated in the manual. This is not all of what the string represents to these people, it also means being demeaned every day of their life, for on their string is a code that says when scanned in the elevator do not allow this stringed person pass the third floor. Or worse yet, do not allow this person to park in the covered paring area. Every day they put on that string they feel like they are being enslaved to the corporation and their higher-ups, and the string makes them want to scream. They say another day of this string and I think I will die, yet they get up and go to work and wear the string, because they really don't know who they are or what they are called to do. The Identity Thief makes them feel like they are living a life of total compromise, and he constantly uses this string to remind them of all they have given up. No wonder when these people go out for lunch, they try to hide their string, they don't want anyone to know that they wear a string.

Near where I live is a giant American corporation. This company I will call the large red wizard is the second largest independent computer software corporation in the world, and they employ thousands of string wearers. About three times a week I ride my bicycle on the trail where many of these string wearers are walking. I have yet to meet a happy string wearer on this trail. As I come upon them on the trail where they are trying to get some sunshine and exercise on their lunch break, I pray for them individually. I have yet to see a smile and very few of them even look at me or answer my hello. These folks are stooped shouldered, sad faced, and I have yet to observe a skip in their step. I feel so sorry for these string wearers, who act as if they will have to spend the afternoon on death row. In the book of Ecclesiastes Chapter 5:19, King Solomon wrote to say that there is nothing better on planet earth than for a person to enjoy their work. The saddest thing about these string wearers is not just that they have such a dread for their work; it is that the Identity Thief has made them to believe that this is who they are. These people get up and dress as a string wearer, go to their string work and they don't just leave it there most of them go home and take out their unhappiness on their husbands, wives and children, all because they are finding their identity in their string.

This problem with the lanyards is no easy problem; everyone in our culture has been entangled by the string in one way or another. The person who loves their string and believes they have found an identity in the string is really in bondage to the string. Even though they might not have to give up this job this person needs to come clean and admit to their string idolatry. They must confess that they have been worshipping at the altar of the corporation and fess up to having a false god. They absolutely must confess that they have been relying on the corporation to meet their needs and not God. They must admit that they have trusted their future to the pension plan and not God. And they must face up to the game playing, the mask wearing and the butt kissing they have done to climb the corporate ladder. This person must realize that they have to get real with God and others if they are going to be living out of a right identity. You simply can't be right if you are not real! Now I am not saying that they have to throw their string away, but they might have to. For certain they will need to put the Identity Thief in his place, by making their colors clear. This doesn't mean that they become a rebel in the work place, or give up being a team player, but they become a real and Spirit filled person who finds their life in Jesus, and not their string.

For the person who absolutely hates their string, they have to approach this situation with a delicate grace. In their hearts they want to tell their bosses to stick this string where the sun doesn't shine, and they have rehearsed their departure speech. But, the Christ following person must realize that they are serving Him and not just the corporation. Even Jesus said give to Caesar what is Caesar's and give to God what belongs to God. So in this imperfect world it is possible to be Spirit filled and totally obedient to Jesus and still wear a string. The key to victory over the string is to realize that the string doesn't make the person, the string is just a corporate necessity and it has nothing to do with your identity. So, affirm that Jesus Christ is your life and true identity, and acknowledge that it is Christ Jesus whom you are serving, and whom you seek to glorify (Colossians 3:24). And then give thanks to God for your string which represents your job and the opportunity you have to serve him in this way. Now throughout your day be in an attitude of prayer, and every time you are reminded about your string tell yourself the truth. It is not your identity, it is not a noose, it is not a ball and chain, it is a tool that I can use, and it represents access to other hearts and souls who need to find life and true identity in Jesus. And if you should ever lose your job for living out of your true identity in Jesus, remember you did not lose your life or your identity, you just lost a string.

We have seen how a badge and a string can instantly be used by the Identity Thief to change how a person thinks about themselves in both the positive and the negative. A uniform has the same kind of magic. Just think of Clark Kent and what happens when he puts on his

Superman uniform, or Spider man, or what happened to Michael Jordan when he laced up his sneakers, or a soldier, or a prisoner. What ever uniform is going over our heads, it has the potential to change us for good or for evil. Think of the person who goes to prison, and in the process they get right with God, yet they have twenty years to wear the stripes or the orange jump suit. That uniform doesn't have to be to them a constant reminder of their failure; it can be their entrance into life-giving ministry with others. I just depends how they respond to the Identity Thief, for he would love to use it to constantly accuse this prisoner of their failure, and bury them in condemnation, he is the accuser of the brothers (Rev. 12:10). Or that uniform can become an invitation to tell the story of God's amazing grace. It all depends if we stiff arm the Identity Thief, and choose to clothe ourselves in the righteousness of Christ, or we let him dress us for failure. We can be dressed for the Lord's glory and success, or dressed for failure depending on how we view the threads we have to wear.

I think it is a wonderful thing when I see a young person wearing an athletic uniform. They have worked hard to earn it and wear it proudly. It is a good thing to see young men hit the weight room in the early mornings all summer long and then earn their school's uniform. And it is a proud moment when you see your team take their field in your school colors and it feels good to yell, "Go big red!" I remember standing on my bench seat crying when my friend George Kyros ran on to the Memorial Stadium field in Lincoln Nebraska as a Cornhusker. I remember running with him in the summer as he trained to compete for our state's pride and joy. If I could have bought a red and white husker football jersey with the number 18 on it I would have. There is both good pride and bad pride and I know in my home town all the athletes started taking pride in their workouts because George was wearing the Nebraska football uniform.

I know lots of people who found their identity in the uniform they once wore. I know a man who can't quit telling stories from his time serving in the Army during World War Two, and every Memorial Day Sunday he still tries to pry himself into his old uniform; it takes a shoe horn. We are so proud of those who served in the greatest generation, and won our freedom, but even this good identity can be a trap for the Identity Thief to use to disguise a theft.

And I know an old Air Force Pilot who won't wear his name or his rank on his old leather bomber jacket and when I ask him why he tells me that was then, and I am going on with my life. What he is trying to say is that today he knows that Jesus Christ is his life and his true identity, and he doesn't want to draw upon a past experience as an identity crutch. He has talked with me about other pilots who always have to put their Air Force stuff on or on display. He thinks it is funny and sad to see guys always living in their past glory. You can spot them: the bumper stickers, the license plate trim, the clothing, and especially the conversations that always start out, "I remember when." Uniforms can be a source of positive pride or they can be a reminder of shame. I remember after the Denver Broncos lost another super bowl. People often forget that this team had been to the dance several times without a win, and after they lost for the third time, I went to the sporting goods store the next day and bought a really nice Bronco sweatshirt for only $5.00. In our culture, when it comes to wearing the uniform, we are only as good as our last game so it is not a good idea to draw our sense of identity from a uniform. The Apostle Paul had some good advice for us when he said, "Rather, clothe yourselves with the Lord Jesus Christ, and do not think about how to gratify the desires of the sinful nature" (Romans 13:14).

Badges, Lanyards (strings), and Uniforms are some ways people find their identity in our culture today. We have been discussing how these things are just temporary and outward symbols but lack true identity power. What I hope is being affirmed is that the only identity that has true significance and lasting power is the name of Jesus, and the good news is that by faith in Him we acquire His wonderful identity as our own.

The other day I was walking in the mall and I noticed a young lady who was wearing pants that were much too tight and riding way too low on her hips. Now please don't ask me why I noticed this, ok? I will tell you I also observed a tattoo on her lower back. I did a double take when I saw this marking because I thought something was crawling down the back of her pants. I didn't ask her what this was all about, but I have come to find out that she was sporting what is called a "Tramp-Stamp." The word tramp used in this way means beggar or vagrant. The word vagrant means a person with no home and no job. And I can only imagine what she is using this tattoo to beg for. So I am left to wonder why in the world would any young lady want to have this meaning stitched with a needle into her skin, permanently inked onto her back, on the small of her back. We have been learning that behavior flows out of identity. I sure hope this young lady doesn't really believe that she is a tramp, a vagrant or a beggar, but she paid some serious coin to make some kind of lasting statement.

I am reminded that we all make mistakes and tattoos can be long lasting visible reminders of some of our mistakes. I think of the young man who had tattooed into his right bicep the name of his girl friend at the time, Barbara, but then he had that name crossed out, and under it he had the name Sally inked in. A few years later he had the name Sally crossed out and the name Rachel was poked in under it. Just a few months later he had Rachel scratched out and under that the artist drilled into his forearm the word "Mom". A few years later he added under the word Mom the name Jesus, who I hope had become his true life and his real identity.

The point I am trying to make is that badges, lanyards, uniforms and tattoos can communicate a lot of things. The Identity Thief will try to get into our heads and hearts with these identity issues, but don't let him. The real mark of a Christian is love, John was a disciple who really loved Jesus and once was called "A Son of Thunder." Maybe he had a thunderbolt tattooed to his bicep? In the gospel he wrote he said this about the true mark of a person who finds their identity in Jesus. He said (speaking for Jesus) "A new command I give you; love one another, as I have loved you, so you must love one another. By this all men will know that you are my disciples, if you love one another" (John 13: 34-35).[11] So, tomorrow morning if you are called to wear the badge, or put a string around your neck, or put on a uniform, make sure you remind yourself that you are loved by

---

[11] To learn more about John, read Book Four, *All We Need to Know* to have Security from Identity Theft. See page 223 in this book.

Jesus Christ, He is your life, and your true identity. Be reminded that His love makes you secure in Him and you do not have to worry or fear what other people think of you. Just walk in the Spirit and let His love flow through you, for this is the true mark of being a Christ follower. If you should be accused of loving in His name or living like He does, consider that to be the highest complement you could ever receive. And if you never hear another human being say words to that effect, just know that if you are truly allowing Jesus to live in you, your heavenly father is cheering you on from heaven, listen close, hear the applause from heaven. He is saying, you are my child, I love you, I am proud of you, I am with you, and I am for you (Zeph. 3:17).

When we truly believe that Jesus Christ is our life and our true identity, His image is engraved in our hearts, and his love naturally flows out of us. This is the true mark of the Christ follower. This makes us "Like a Rock" and gives us security from identity theft.

Chapter 11
THE MARK

John 13:34-35

I haven't met anyone who has disliked Dr. Seuss; I especially liked his children's story about Sneetchland. You probably remember how there were Star Belly Sneetches and there were Plain Belly Sneetches. We learned about prejudice because the Star Belly Sneetches flaunted their superior mark and snubbed the Plain Belly Sneetches. Then along came a capitalist named McBean who developed a Star-on-star-off machine. This changed the landscape of Sneetchland and the original Star Bellies shelled out cash to become Plain Bellies. And then you scratch your head and think, who was content in their identity? You realize that is was McBean who was making off with the cash. Isn't that how it is? I used to have hair, now I am really glad I don't have hair. But, there were a lot of "Hair-club-for-men" advertisements dropped off on my desk when I was a teacher. Today, there are marks tattoos, and piercings people desire on their bodies, and I think McBean is the only one who ends up happy. Even the Bible discusses the mark that makes our identity secure in God.

In Genesis 17 God makes a covenant with Abraham that involved a cutting mark, as a sign of relationship/identity with Him. He said, "You are to undergo circumcision, and it will be a sign of the Covenant between me and you. For the generations to come every male among you who is eight days old must be circumcised, including those born in your household or bought with money from a foreigner—those who are not your offspring. My covenant in your flesh is to be an everlasting covenant (Genesis 17: 12 & 14).

This mark seems rather unusual from my male point of view. Why couldn't God have made the mark a particular hair style, you know, like the "southern evangelist's poof"? Why did he have to touch the private part of a man? Maybe there is a reason for this. Some have speculated that this cut was to be a reminder to every man of God about his responsibility to live chaste, respectful and above reproach sexually. It is audacious to me to know that men have a tendency to find their identity in that part of their anatomy, thinking that part is their core. I'll tell it to you straight, if that is all there is to a man, he is shallow. How a man conducts himself sexually is a determinate about his identity. And God gives the man this reminder that he is to be holy, and clean. So some experts suggest that there were also sanitary reasons for this mark; God was both keeping His people holy and healthy.

In Dr. Suess's Star Belly story, it wouldn't be long before God's men started finding their identity in their circumcision this physical mark and in their religion, and not in God alone. I know this sounds very strange, but people have a tendency to be outward focused. I Samuel 16 says, "Man looks to the outward appearance, but God looks to the heart." This problem doesn't just affect men, I know women who have had a few bad hair days, and they will spend hundreds of dollars to make their hair work for them. Peter had to write and say to some women, "Your beauty should not come from outward adornment, such as braided hair and the wearing of gold jewelry and fine clothes. Instead it should be that of your inner self, the unfading beauty of a gentle and quiet spirit, which is of great worth in God's sight" (I Peter 3:3-4). Our culture is so outward focused you would think McBean runs the world.

Perhaps the most powerful identity passage in the Bible is the Apostle Paul's found in Romans 2:25-29 where is says, "Circumcision has value if you observe the law, but if you break the law, you have become as though you had not been circumcised. If those who are not circumcised keep the law's requirements, will they not be regarded as though they were circumcised? The one who is not circumcised physically yet obeys the law will condemn you who, even though you have the written code and circumcision, are a law breaker. A man is not a Jew if he is only one outwardly, nor is circumcision merely outward and physical. No, a man is a Jew is he is one inwardly; and circumcision is circumcision of the heart, by the Spirit, not by the written code. Such a man's praise is not from men but from God." In this text the Apostle points to God's original aim, in circumcision, God always uses the physical to make a spiritual point. In other words God touched a man's private part to get to his heart. And you thought the way to a man's heart was through his stomach. The fishermen have it right when they say, "a way to a man's heart is through his fly."

As in this passage the Apostle moves us from religion to a very personal faith. And I add, he is getting very personal, and every man agrees. Paul simply relates that if our religion is that of checking off lists, keeping the rules, and meeting the law's requirements, we don't understand the heart of God. God made us for Himself, He wants to know us, walk with us, talk with us, He wants to be our God and He want us to love Him with our heart. Religion by its emphasis on the outward and the rules can make for a cold, distant, and cruel life. Remember how Paul was once the religious Saul who found his identity in his law-keeping and religious striving? He was so advanced in his Pharisaic religious climb that he had become like the Muslim extremist who would strap on a bomb and go blow people up in the name of their religion. So please know God's goal for our lives has nothing to do with religion.

God stated His goal clearly in Deuteronomy 30:6 when he said, "The Lord your God will circumcise your hearts and the hearts of your descendents, so that you may love Him with all your heart and with all your soul and live." So we get the hint, that God is looking to the heart, and that a real man to Him is a man who knows how to love Him. Jesus said, "A new command I give you; love one another, as I have loved you, so you must love one another. By this all men will know that you are my disciples, if you love one another" (John 13:34-35). This love is the "mark" of a follower of Jesus. And the real identity issue for us is, are we a Jew inwardly? Do we have love for God and people in our hearts? To have this love we have to have hearts that have been "cut", or circumcised. So, we must ask, how do we get this mark? And how do we draw our identity from God and get our praise from Him?

The scriptures are so good at explaining this delicate subject, As Paul further explains this in Ephesians 2:11, "Therefore, remember that formerly you who are Gentiles by birth and called "uncircumcised" by those who call themselves the circumcision" (that done in the body by the hands of men), remember that at that time you were separate from Christ, excluded from citizenship in Israel and foreigners to the covenants of the promise, without hope and without God in the world." Just as Star Bellies was a story of identity, Paul asserts that Gentiles because they are 'uncircumcised, and without a relationship with God, didn't have a meaningful identity. He couldn't be more clear, he says the words: separate, excluded, without hope, and without God.

The Text continues by saying, "But now in Christ Jesus you who once were far away have been brought near through the blood of Christ." Now we can get excited here, as rejected people become belongers, and near people through the blood of Christ. And just as blood/DNA gives a person a physical identity, we see that the blood of Jesus is what makes us into people with a beautiful identity.

Paul continues to expound, "For He Himself is our peace, who has made the two one and has destroyed the barrier, the dividing wall of hostility, by abolishing in his flesh, the law with its commandments and regulations. His purpose was to create in Himself one new man out of the two, thus making peace, and in this one body to reconcile both of them to God through the cross, by which He put to death their hostility" (2:14). In this text we get a Grace River illustration, as there was a separation between Jews and Gentiles much like there are people standing on the Mt.Truth side of the River, and there are people stranded in the sandy banks of discipline, the point is neither of them are *in* the river. From the cross of Jesus not only flowed His blood, but this is where the river of Grace begins, and unity is found as we drop our rocks and embrace each other in the river of God's grace. It is here we can bask in God's unconditional acceptance and experience this oneness; we are in this one river by grace alone. It doesn't matter if you were previously a Jew or a Gentile; we are nothing if we are not in the River of God's Grace.[12]

Paul explains how we can experience unity and identity in Grace River, the text continues, "by abolishing in His flesh the law with its commandments and regulations. His purpose was to create in Himself one new man out of the two, thus making peace, and in one this one

---

[12] See Appendix #2, p. 220, The Grace River Model.

body to reconcile both of them to God through the cross, by which He put to death their hostility" (Ephesians 2:15-16). This passage really is the hope of our world today because only when religious people find their identity in Jesus, and the irreligious people need to know that that they are welcome to enter this River of Grace Jesus offers also.

We need to help people everywhere realize the power of the cross and the blood of Jesus. For, here is where people can die to self, sin and religion and be reconciled to God and each other. But, if our identity is found in the "6-Ps": power, possessions, pleasure, popularity, prestige or physical appearance (7 if we include philosophy). These prideful "Ps" hinder the possibility of unity, they keep people separated out from each other and make peace with God impossible. The good-news is that the cross compels humility by getting us to realize that God loves us even while we were yet in a sinning state (Romans 5:8). There is unity in Grace River because both the Jew and the Gentile can come into the water of God's grace with an attitude of gratitude, realizing we/they have a new identity in Jesus only.

The Apostle explained this miracle by saying, "He came and preached peace to you who were far away and peace to those who were near. For through Him we both have access to the Father by one Spirit. Consequently, you are no longer foreigners and aliens, but fellow citizens with God's people and members of God's household, built on the foundation of the apostles and prophets, with Christ Jesus Himself as the chief Cornerstone" (Ephesians 2:17-20). Through the foolishness of preaching our identities were changed! Those who were near were the Jews, and the Gentiles were far away, but now we can be brothers and sisters and truly close to God and each other by realizing that the same Spirit that resides in a converted Jew is the same Spirit who is in a converted Gentile. The only way, we have this new life is because we were born-again by the Holy Spirit (John 3:1-3). And because of this miracle we now have the best identity possible; we are members of God's household, we are COGs, Children of God!

"With God as our father, brothers all are we". Those are the words of a song I sang in the late 60's and early 70's as peace was such a idealistic expression back then, but this miracle can be our reality through Jesus Christ. And because of this unity Paul concludes this section of scripture with a marvelous prayer, "For this reason I kneel before the Father, from whom his whole family in heaven and on earth derives its name. I pray that out of His glorious riches, He may strengthen you with power through His Spirit in your inner being so that Christ may dwell in your hearts through faith. And I pray that you being rooted and established in love may have power together with all the saints to grasp how wide and long and high and deep is the love of Christ, and to know this love that surpasses knowledge—that you may be filled to the measure of all the fullness of God." Wow, what a prayer! Do you see the emphasis on your identity in Jesus?

This unity is not the result of a physical mark on our bodies. The Star Bellies and the Plain Bellies never experienced this contented unity in one new man, the man Jesus. He makes it clear that this is the result of the work of the Holy Spirit who, has circumcised and transformed each believers heart. After He "cut" the hardness out of our hearts, He makes room for Himself.

Galatians 5:22 says, "the fruit of the Spirit is love" and now each Christ follower has this indelible mark, Love is the fruit of the Spirit and the mark of a real Christian.

Paul confirms this in Galatians 5:6, "For in Christ Jesus neither circumcision nor uncircumcision has any value. The only thing that counts is faith expressing itself in love." Here Paul had once prided himself in his external mark, and now he knows what God wanted all along, a circumcised heart, a heart that was new and could love and care for the heart of God and people (Ezekiel 36:26).

I bet you, like me, had no idea this issue of circumcision was such an identity issue in the scriptures. Thank the Good Lord that we are not under that covenant today and I like our culture better. However the application is obvious, many of us are so external and outward focused. Sometimes we act like we need stars on our bellies, or then we need a plain belly. After we come to our senses and put the insanity aside we by the grace of God realize all we really need is a circumcised heart, and real love in our lives! This is the true mark that is engraved on our hearts; this is the mark that gives our lives meaning. For with out love we know we are nothing! (I Corinthians 13).

Concluding Scripture:

When you were dead in your sins and in the uncircumcision
Of your sinful nature, God made you alive with Christ,
He forgave all our sins,
Having canceled the written code, with its regulations, that was
Against us; He took it away, nailing it to the cross.
Colossians 2:14

Here there is no Greek, or Jew,
Circumcised or uncircumcised, barbarian,
Scythian, slave or free, but Christ is all, and is in all.
Colossians 3:11

When we learn to live with this understanding we have security from identity theft, and can be "Like a Rock."

Chapter 12
COVENANT IDENTITY

Hebrews 8-11

Susie Brown had been reading BRIDES Magazine since she was old enough to read, and she would dream about her special day. When she was with her girl friends they would play dress up and their favorite script to act out was of the wedding day. When Bobby Armstrong who had been dating her for more than a year popped the question, and placed that stone on her ring finger, Susie felt so complete. Where ever she went she would dangle that sparkling ring out for everyone to gawk about, and they would talk about her big day and her new identity.

I know a woman who coached her daughters to know that they could marry more money in fifteen minutes than they could make in a lifetime. It is true, that after you say I do and sign that Marriage Covenant your life changes in a dramatic way. Women experience joy beyond measure because they are so satisfied by being united with a man and love taking on his name, and find their identity in this covenant. And there are women who are so disappointed in their new identity and ashamed of their husband they wish they had never said I do because this decision has had such a negative impact on them.

A covenant, a will, and a contract are such powerful tools a person can draw their identity from them. We all know of people who are so esteemed because they are listed in their families will, and their inheritance will be so significant that they and others think, wow, they really are somebody. And there is the person who has signed the contract to work for the big corporation with all the benefits of retirement, health insurance, a car and a parking space to go with it. That person has signed up for a life-time of service and many who sign these contracts also take on the corporation as their identity. They wear the logos on their hats and shirts, and even see their life in relation to their position with the corporation.

God is a covenant making and a covenant keeping God. The Old Testament part of the Bible is really about the old Covenants God made with His people. And the New Testament part of the Bible is about the new Covenant God made with his people. In both parts of the Bible God's children found their identity in relation to this covenant, the covenant showed the world and the Children of God how special they were. And just as an engaged woman would walk around showing off her engagement ring to say, "See I am somebody", God's children have always made their boast and found their identity in the covenant.

Some of the Old Covenants were "conditional" covenants, where God said if you do your part, then I will do my part. But, if you fail, there are consequences. While the New Covenant is a perfect and unconditional covenant, in that God basically states that He will complete both the human and the God side of this agreement. Charles Haddan Spurgeon, the great preacher of yesteryear (1830's), said this about the old Covenants, "the old covenant was founded on the principle of merit. Essentially, the covenant conditions were these, "serve God, and you will be rewarded for it; if you walk perfectly in the fear of the Lord, God will deal with you, and all the blessings of Mount Gerizim (Deut. 11:29, 27:12) will come upon you, and you will be exceedingly blessed in this world and in the world to come."

These Old Covenants were clear, they said if you obey, I will bless and if you disobey there will be a curse. These conditional covenants give reason for so many having a conditional identity today. People reason, if I do well then I am good and I am blessed. But, if I fail, then I am a failure and I am cursed. We need a better covenant and a better way to find a perpetually positive identity! In the Garden of Eden God gave to Adam and Eve the conditions of the tree, "if you eat from the tree of the Knowledge of Good and evil, there will be a curse on you." We all know and experience the consequences of this failure as Adam and Eve representatively have communicated to all us these negative consequences.

Through Moses God gave mankind strict and very conditional covenants. We are all familiar with the Ten Commandments that have served us well with clear boundaries, but they also condemn us because we fail them in many ways. God also gave us ordinances and judgments that placed responsibility on His people to meet the conditions in order to have His blessing. Though there is holiness and righteousness in these covenants, but there is also a heavy dose of bad news. The Bad news is the realization of our failure to live with in these God ordained boundaries, and the judgmental consequences.

The Old Testament also serves as a preview of coming attractions because there are some unconditional Covenants that show us some of the grace that will be revealed in the grace filled New Covenant in the Blood of Jesus Christ. God promised Noah and his sons His grace by saying, "I will establish my covenant with you: Never again will all life be cut off by the waters of a flood; never again will there be a flood to destroy the earth. And God said this is a sign of the covenant I am making between me and you and every living creature with you, a covenant for all generations to come: I have set my rainbow in the clouds, and it will be a sign of the covenant between me and the earth" (Genesis 9:9-13).

This is a beautiful picture of the grace that is to come; God says of His beautiful rainbow that it will serve as reminder of the covenant He has made. We get a glimmer of grace here because there is absolutely nothing we humans can do to keep this contract. This rainbow covenant is all on God; He has promised not to destroy us and regularly reminds us of this covenant by placing a beautiful rainbow in the sky to restate His grace toward us. There are people who try to explain away the rainbow with scientific research; I choose to be reminded of God's grace and His unconditional love!

God also gave a covenant to Abraham and to David to show case His unconditional love. God told Abraham in his old age that the whole world would be blessed through Him. Granted, his faith was tested, but this covenant was unconditional and God gave Abraham and Sarah a blessed son named Isaac. Though Abraham was tested again and again, this unconditional promise has blessed the entire world with the nation of Israel and the savior of the world Jesus Christ.

And to David God promises a forever kingdom as a result of His unconditional love. God spoke this unconditional covenant and promise to David through Nathan, "The Lord declares to you that the Lord Himself will establish a house for you: When your days are over and you rest with your fathers, I will raise up your offspring to succeed you, who will come from your own body, and I will establish His kingdom. He is the one who will build a house for my name, and I will establish the throne of His kingdom forever. I will be His father and He will be my son. When he does wrong, I will punish him with the rod of men, with floggings inflicted by men. But my love will never be taken from him, as I took it away from Saul, whom I removed from before you. Your house and your kingdom will endure forever before me; your throne will be established forever" (2 Samuel 7:14-16).

In this difficult passage we see God promising an unending royal linage, a throne and a kingdom that is forever. And in this passage we get a prophetic picture of how Jesus, the perfect and sinless Lamb of God would become sin and an acceptable substitute for you and me. And Just as Adam as a representative for you and me and all man kind imparted to us the consequences of sin, Jesus the second Adam who never sinned would become sin, would "do wrong" so we could be made righteous by His once for all sacrifice. And as our representative we now can receive God's unconditional love through His blood that was shed in this new covenant in His blood.

My favorite New Testament/covenant passage is 2 Corinthians 5:21 as tells of our Covenant identity in Jesus, "God made Him who had no sin to be sin for us, so that we might become the righteousness of God." This passage explains the Old Testament sacrificial system, the people of God would have to bring an unblemished animal to the priests in the temple and offer it up as a sacrifice and the blood would be shed to temporarily cover their sins. The New Testament is about the New Covenant in the blood of Jesus, a once for all and all time sacrifice that can bring people into the unconditional love and perpetual of God.

The Ministry of Jesus is explained by the writer of the book of Hebrews, and he tells us how much better this New Covenant is, "but the ministry Jesus has received is superior to the old one, and it is founded on better promises. For if there had been nothing wrong with that first covenant, no place would have been sought for another. But God found fault with the people and said, "the time is coming, declares the Lord, when I will make a new covenant with the house of Israel and with the house of Judah" (Hebrews 8:6-8).

This text makes a claim of being a superior covenant, but the question is: who is this superior for? The answer is for both God and His children. For God, because it now makes it possible for nothing to interfere with His desire to have relationship with His children everywhere. Prior to this New Covenant God's conditions and his holiness/righteousness prevented unhindered relationship. God had to keep his word, and His Holy/righteous character couldn't just overlook sin and disobedience. Sin and disobedience always had to be taken care of, and in this New Covenant Jesus takes care of the sin and disobedience problems. So this new covenant is better for both God and us.

Our Covenant identity is secured by Jesus when God says, "This covenant I will make with the house of Israel after that time declares the Lord. I will put my laws on their minds and write them on their hearts. I will be their God and they will be my people." (Hebrews 8:10). God's desire is fulfilled, His desire for a forever family and relationship with His children is now possible. And our identity needs are now secured because God becomes our God! He through this new Covenant can become our personal God.

So by having God as our God we are secure. His position and his attributes are ours, if we by faith are partakers of this New Covenant. So now with God as our Father and King we now have a royal identity. And with Him as our Sovereign and Ruler we are now included in his dominion. Consider His attributes:[13]

His Love makes us secure (Romans 8:37-39)

God is Holy: Now by faith we are holy (Romans 5:1)

God is Omnipotent (all powerful): Now we have His power to live this new life, we are empowered by His Holy Spirit (Acts 1:8)

God is omniscient (all knowing): Now we have the mind of Christ and can know His ways.

God is Omnipresent (everywhere present): Now we can enjoy abiding in His presence wherever we are, and He has promised to never leave us (Hebrews 13:5)

---

[13] See Chapter 15, "The Attributes of God 'Rock' our Identity", p. 155 in this book, for a deeper study on this powerful way to affirm our identity in God.

God is eternal (not bounded by time): Now we have our eternity securely assured in Him and we no longer have to live like this earthly life is all there is (1 John 5:11-15)

God is generous. He is a giving God (John 3:16). Therefore we can be rivers, and not reservoirs, and release His blessings to others. Being a giver is now our identity.

God is Just: (He does what is morally right). Now we can trust Him to work out the details of our lives. We do not have to try to manipulate a thing, we will just trust and obey and leave the results with Him. We will not be preoccupied with "fair", we know nothing is fair, but we trust that God is good and just and will work everything out in His time and in His way.

Our Covenant identity includes knowing God in His attributes! To get to know Him and who we are in Him, we should regularly meditate on His names and attributes because this exercise will build us up in our true identity in God. Remember He says, "and I will be their God."

God helps us to understand our New Covenant identity when He says, "I will put my laws on their minds, and write them on their hearts" (Romans 2:15). Knowing what God has done here is a powerful way to beat back the Devil. I think the Devil tries to intimidate with God's Word. We look at it the Bible and think it is a huge book, I can never understand it! It's big, thick and written in a weird religious language, and talks about things from another time and culture. Those are thoughts straight from hell; they are an effective satanic deception.

God's Word is simple, clear, and easy to understand. It is mostly a story format, with some history, wisdom, prophetic, and legal language. The good-news here is that God in His wisdom repeats these stories, several times and retells most of it over and over so in reality it isn't as big as it appears. And on top of this simple understanding He puts what we need to know in our minds and writes His laws on our hearts. And Jesus sums up His laws by saying, "Love the Lord your God with all your heart and with all your soul and with all your mind.' This is the first and the greatest commandment. And the second like it: 'love your neighbor like yourself.' All the law and the prophets hang on these two commandments" (Matthew 22:37-40). So in the New

Covenant we find a beautiful simplicity.

I tried to read the Bible before I truly believed in Jesus. To me it was mumbo-jumbo, I didn't understand it, and couldn't concentrate upon it. But, when I believed in Jesus, the Holy Spirit entered my life, and gave me understanding, and illumination. It was as if the lights came on, and I could see what God was saying. I couldn't put it down. To this day I don't know how I passed those first two years of college because I spent a lot of my free time reading the Bible. What I had thought was a mystical message became to me a personal love-letter as he helped me get to know His Word. He promises to do this work in our minds and hearts to help us understand His ways. He promised Jeremiah in the Old Testament, "I will give them a heart to know me, that I am the Lord. They will be my people and I will be their God, for they will return to me with all their heart" (Jeremiah 24:7). And Ezekiel wrote, "I will give you a new heart and put a new spirit in you; I will remove from you your heart of stone and give you a heart of flesh. I will put my Spirit in you and move you to follow my decrees and be careful to keep my laws" (Ezekiel 36:26). So, in this marvelous New Covenant Identity of ours God not only keeps both sides of the deal but works inside of us to assure us in our minds and hearts that we are His and walking in His ways. And He gives us a new mind so we can know Him. A new heart so we can love him and a new will so we want to and are able to obey Him. He covers it all!

This New Covenant is not about knowing every jot and title of God's Old Testament laws and decrees, it is about knowing Him. David knew of this when he wrote the 23rd Psalm. He knew he was secure, simply because he knew the shepherd, and in the New Covenant we see that Jesus is the Good Shepherd, who gave His life for the sheep (Do you know who you are?). John would say, "And this is eternal life, that we may know Him" (John 17:3). So, to make this clear it is not what we know it is who we know and if we know the Shepherd, we are in good shape and our identity is as secure as the Shepherds because we are in Him and he is in us. His life is ours and so is His identity. How secure do you think Jesus is? Isn't He the most secure person ever? And now by faith we are in Him!

In Hebrews 8: 11-12 makes knowing Him the central issue of this

New Covenant Identity. "No longer will a man teach his neighbor, or a man his brother, saying 'know the lord' because they all will know me, from the least of them to the greatest. For I will forgive their wickedness and will remember their sins no more." How good it is to know there is no ranking of status in God's family, the joy is in knowing Him, and you can't have a better identity than this. And to top it off, all our sins are forgiven and remembered no more. So why do we sometimes feel shame and guilt? (Read on finish this book, for freedom sake, Grace River is the way of freedom)

But, before we start doing handsprings and somersaults, let's grasp the significance of the New Covenant in the blood of Christ. Hebrews 9:11-12 says, "When Christ came as high Priest of the good things that are already here, he went through the greater and more perfect tabernacle that is not man-made, that is to say, not part of this creation. He did not enter by means of blood of goats and calves; but he entered the most Holy place once for all by his own blood having obtained eternal redemption." So it is His blood that was the purchase price of our redemption. Let me explain, to redeem means to buy out of bondage. We were in bondage to sin, Satan and this world, and just as you go to the grocery store to buy out of that store your food with hard earned money. Jesus bought you out of bondage with the price of His blood. Value is usually determined by the price that is paid. So your value and identity is of great value to God because the highest of all prices was paid. More than great diamonds, or famous paintings or fabulous cars. You are valued by God so much that Jesus spent His blood, and gave his life for you.

Even though we know that we are of great value and have a powerful identity we can still feel crummy inside our souls. But, God even took care of this problem through the New Covenant in the blood of Jesus. In Hebrews 9:14 we read, "how much more, then, will the blood of Christ, who through eternal Spirit offered himself unblemished to God, cleanse our consciences from acts that lead to death, so that we may serve the Living God." Many of us might know the truth about who Jesus is and what He accomplished with His blood, but still be stagnant and in bondage to the shame and guilt of our life. And Satan is quick to remind you of past failures because he is the "accuser of the brothers". (Revelation 12:10). But, choose to believe Jesus can constantly be renewing your conscience and easing our so we can live with ourselves. His presence in us is the key to winning the war within us. Because in His presence is peace, joy, hope and encouragement.

Spurgeon was able to sum this New Covenant up by saying, "Christ was to come into the world and perfectly obey the divine law. Inasmuch as the first Adam had broken the law, He was to suffer the penalty of sin. If He would do both of these, then all whom He represented would be blessed in His blessedness and be saved because of His merit. Do you see that, until our Lord lived and died on this earth, it was a covenant of works on His part? He has certain works to perform; upon condition of His performance, certain blessings would be given to us" (God's Grace to You, C. H. Spurgeon, p. 9).

Jesus has done it all, he has lived the perfect life, kept all the commands, was obedient to death, and allowed Himself to be nailed to the cross so his blood would flow and cleanse us of all our wrongs. He then rose from the dead to give us the assurance this covenant is for real, and ascended into Heaven so the Holy Spirit would come and secure us and seal us with our true identity as blood bought children of God (Romans 8).

God has pledged to give all of us unmerited favor and a covenant Identity by believing in the works of Jesus. There is nothing we can do but believe and say thank you, for in doing this we express our faith in Him and show that we know Him and want to know Him better.

The moment we have the blood of Christ applied to our lives, whether by saying thank you, or by crying out to him in sorrow for our sins, at this moment we passed from the curse, through the cross and into the full acceptance and blessings of God. At this moment we became a holy, heir of everything that belongs to Jesus. For, now He is our life and all that is His, He has given to us. Paul called this being a "joint-heir", as He has given you everything, Even Covenant Identity.

Meditate on these 33 blessings that instantly became ours as we became a partaker of A Covenant Identity by believing in the blood of Jesus.

Our regular meditation of these truths will help us renew our minds and live out of our true identity in Jesus (Make each of these statements into a thank you prayer to God. Try to make this exercise even more personal by changing the words to: Thank you God that I am_____!). Review the following 33 benefits in this exercise.

This is a powerful way to allow the Holy Spirit to "engrave" these truths in our hearts and minds!

COVENANT BENEFITS

THE BENEFITS OF OUR IDENTITY IN JESUS

1. We are part of the eternal plan of God (1 Peter 1:2,20)
2. We are redeemed! (Galatians 5:1, Romans 3:24)
3. We are reconciled to God! (II Corinthians 5:17-19)
4. We have a living relationship with God (1 John 2:2-11)
5. We are forgiven (Romans 8:1, Hebrews 4:16)
6. We have been placed in Christ (mentioned over 150 times in the New Testament)
7. We are free from the law (Romans 6:14, 7:6, 8:2-3)
8. We are children of God (Ephesians 2:11-13, Galatians 3:26)
9. We are adopted and have son ship (Ephesians 1:1-5)
10. We are made acceptable to God! (Ephesians 1:4, 1 Peter 2:5, Romans 12:1-3)
11. We are justified, that means we have been legally declared righteous, and enjoy peace with God (Romans 5:1)
12. We have been brought near to God (Ephesians 2:12-13)
13. We have been delivered from the power of darkness (Colossians 1:13)
14. We have entered the kingdom of God (I Thessalonians 2:12)
15. Our lives are now established on the Rock, Christ Jesus (Matt. 7:24-27, 1 Cor. 3:9)
16. We are a gift from the Father to the Son (John 17)
17. We have had our hearts circumcised in Christ (Romans 2:28-29, Col. 2:11)

18. We are partakers of the divine nature and the royal priesthood (2 Peter 1:4, 1 Peter 2:5-9)
19. We are a chosen generation, a holy nation, a people who belong to God (1 Peter 2:9)
20. We have our citizenship in heaven (Philippians 3:20, 1 Peter 2:11)
21. We belong in the family and household of God (Galatians 6:10)
22. We enjoy fellowship with the saints (1 Corinthians 12)
23. We have a heavenly association (Hebrews 12:1-2)
24. We enjoy constant access to God (Hebrews 4:16)
25. We are in the "much more" care of God (Matthew 6:26)
26. We have an inheritance! (Ephesians 1:18)
27. We share in the inheritance with the saints (1 Peter 1:4, Colossians 3:1-4)
28. We now live as children of the light (Ephesians 5:8, 1 John 1:7)
29. We have a relationship with the Holy Spirit (Romans 8:9)
30. We are now able to manifest the "fruit of the Spirit" (Galatians 5:22-23)
31. We are being sanctified, and we shall be glorified (John 17:17, Romans 8:18-30)
32. We are complete in Him! (Colossians 2:9-10, 2 Peter 1:3)
33. We possess every spiritual blessing (Ephesians 1:3) (adapted from Lewis Sperry Chafers SYSTEMATIC THEOLOGY VOL III)

Another way to strengthen our resolve to live our Covenant identity is by listening to and meditating on great music. Look at these words from Stuart Townsend and Keith Getty, their song is called, "IN CHRIST ALONE:"

In Christ alone my hope is found
He is my light, my strength, my song
This cornerstone, this solid ground
Firm through the fiercest drought and storm…

What heights of love, what depths of peace
When fears are stilled and striving cease
My comforter, my All-in-All
Here in the love of Christ I stand...

No guilt in life, no fear in death
This is the power of Christ in me
From life's first cry to final breath
Jesus commands my destiny...

In covenant we find our identity and destiny. A great way to be reminded of this truth and to experience this more fully is to worship God in singing these great thoughts back to Him. When David experienced so much warfare, he won the battles by worshipping God. It was in these moments he saw God as his Rock, and knew that he was secure in his identity in Him, because of God, he was "Like a Rock."

Chapter 13
IDENTITY IN COMMUNION

Finding our identity in the Lord's Supper

Luke 22:19-26

In the sacraments of Baptism and the Lord's Supper the Jesus follower can connect His/her identity to Jesus in several ways. In Baptism we clearly identify with Jesus death, burial and resurrection through the symbolism of water. By going under the water we get a picture of going into the death of the abyss, and coming up out of the water gives us a clear resurrection vision. I love seeing immersion baptisms and witnessing the expressions on peoples faces as they come out of the water and are reminded to "walk in newness of life." This is a wonderful life-giving symbol of how the believer personally identities with Jesus through the obedience of baptism. The Lord's Supper (commonly called Communion) is also a great privilege for the believer to identify with Jesus in the elements of the bread and the cup and what they mean.

Our Lord Jesus is the Master teacher, and He has given us this Lord's Supper to be perpetually practiced in our church fellowships. We are instructed to remember who He is, what He has done and who we are in Him. This sacrament shows the significance of God becoming a man, and the purpose of His sacrificial death on the cross. It emphasizes the blood of Christ as the central feature of the new covenant, but it also causes us to remember the many ways Jesus identified with us in body and soul through the bread. This memorial has been a meaningful experience and an identification experience for millions of Christ followers since Jesus served it.

It is interesting to note that the first Lord's Supper Jesus shared with His disciples happened during Passover week. Jesus especially planned this experience so has to help his disciples make the connection between the blood of the Lamb and their salvation. Remember during the time Israel was in slavery in Egypt, and Moses pleaded with the Pharaoh to "let my people go"? Remember how

Pharaoh's heart was so hard, but after ten plagues he relented and God's people were delivered from this terrible bondage through the power of the blood. On the tenth plague, God caused death to spread throughout the land, but He had promised his children if they would put the blood of a lamb on their door posts, death would Passover them, hence we are under the blood and now we have a meaningful Passover celebration for God's children everywhere.

In the context of this Lamb-selection week when God's children would go to Jerusalem and select their lamb for the sacrifice, Jesus had an intimate meal with His disciples where he essentially told them that He was the once for all time Lamb of God that had been selected for sacrifice on Friday. Jesus really couldn't have been clearer, but because of all the festivities and the quickly changing tone of the week-end many of them would miss what he was saying to them about His identity and theirs in Him seen in this Lord's Supper.

It is important to see how God the Father set up this awesome illustration for us with the use of the unleavened bread. Jesus uses a very physical illustration to make a spiritual point. In Egypt they didn't have time to let the bread rise before they began their trek. And what a physical undertaking it was! Can you imagine transporting all the people, and the animals, and their possessions? Certainly God, who had just protected and released them by their being under the blood, would help them make it to the Promised Land. So, the bread was a common way of relating to life in a physical way. And just as bread is a powerful representation of a complete food, (fiber, protein, and carbohydrate). Jesus would use bread to help His disciples see that He was the complete fulfillment of prophecy and all that we need to live in God's promises.

On the Passover evening Jesus has set up a fellowship gathering in a furnished upper room. In Luke 22:19 the scripture says, "And He took bread, gave thanks and broke it, and gave it to them, saying, "This is my body given for you; do this in remembrance of me." And as the disciples held that physical piece of bread in their hands, they were humbled by all the physical ways Jesus came to be with them. Some of them were starting to understand that Jesus was "God with them", the manna or the bread from heaven.

It was predicted in advance that He would be called Emmanuel which means "God with us." Did they understand the symbolism? His mother Mary knew of Jesus in a very physical way. She carried Him, birthed him and nursed him as an ordinary human baby yet He was the God-man. He in all reality was the bread or the manna from heaven, a supernatural provision from God. Jesus did miracles with bread; He fed thousands by taking a few fish and loaves of bread. I think some of the disciples were starting to get the picture. I am sure they had heard how the Spirit of God took Jesus out to the desert to be tempted by the devil, and there the devil really smacked Him with an identity attack. He said to Jesus after Jesus had fasted for forty days and He was physically very hungry, "if you are the Son of God command these stones to become bread." But Jesus, even though He felt fully human hunger pangs, was able to defer to the scriptures and answer, "It is written: 'Man does not live on bread alone, but on every word that comes from the mouth of God" (Matthew 4:4).

From the picture of the bread we get a very earthy and physical understanding of how Jesus has identified with us. We all are tempted in many ways, and we see how Jesus was tempted in the physical. We also see how Jesus healed the man who was born blind in a very earthy way; He spit, made a mud cake from the dirt and puttied up his eyes, and healed him. And speaking of dirt, Jesus would take a towel and a wash basin and wash the disciple's feet. Peter, probably being embarrassed by his "toe jam," said, well, then wash all of me. There were certainly some good laughs while these disciples experienced Jesus is a physical, earthy and human way. But nothing would come close to the physical and soulish pain Jesus was about to experience on his way to the cross.

Jesus said as he held out the bread, "this is my body." All we have to do is remember the movie THE PASSION OF THE CHRIST. From memory we can recall how Jesus was torn up by the torture. But, don't think it was just physical pain. His soul was being wrecked and abandonment was killing him because his disciples would leave Him, and he was betrayed. Have you ever experienced the pain of betrayal? His mind and emotions were overloaded with the pressures of the trial, the crowds, and the weight of all eternity. And then there was the weight of sin on him. All of yours and all of mine was on Him when he was nailed to the cross. And think about what happened to his ligaments, tendons, arteries and bones as was raised up on that cross. He was really being torn up for us. Then the sky turned black and He felt the separation from His Father, and I agree with the Apostles Creed that Jesus descended into hell and experienced the depths of depravity.

There is even more to be said about the bread. But, let's think about our identity and the significance of saying thanks. Jesus knew how this week end's festivities were going to end up for Him. He knew the hosanna, chants and celebratory cheers would quickly turn in to cries of "crucify Him" and He would be unjustly tried, unmercifully mocked, and then scourged with a leather whip called the "cat of nine tails", thirty nine times and have His skin, tissue, fat and muscle torn from His back and then He would be nailed to the rough wooden cross and suffer a Roman crucifixion. But, before all of this He gave thanks even knowing what was going to happen. He gave thanks because this was His purpose and this is His true identity. He is the savior of the world who came to die for our sins.

Jesus, because He lived out of His true identity, was able to give thanks and the writer of the book of Hebrews said, "who for the joy set before Him endured the cross, despising its shame, and sat down at the right hand of the throne of God."(Hebrews 12:2-3). Living out his Covenant and Communion identity Jesus was able to give thanks because He knew what this bread and the cup meant, it meant our forgiveness and acceptance. And when we know we are living out of a strong identity, fully forgiven and completely accepted in the Beloved we too can despise shame and stand up against great pressures.

He gave thanks even though He knew He was about to become sin for us. Even though Jesus is God and is pure, holy, righteous and a blameless He was going to die as a sinner. Remember how His religious enemies couldn't even find fault in Him. In the cross Jesus would become our sin offering, He was the Lamb of God on the altar that afternoon, and the soldiers, the crowd, and bystanders were witnessing the Passover Sacrifice. And God was satisfying the righteous requirements of His holiness by having sin punished and atoned for. God's anger against us and our sins was being drained by Jesus blood flowing freely from his veins. God's anger against us is now and forever appeased if we believe in the power of the blood of Jesus. The Apostle Paul put it this way, "God made Him who had no sin to be sin for us, so that in Him we might become the righteousness of God" (2 Corinthians 5:21).

Our Identity is found in this Communion, or Eucharist meal. The Bread and the Cup shows us our identity, because by faith in what Jesus has done represented in these elements our identity is changed. We are transferred from darkness to light, from death to life, from sinner to saint, from unrighteous to the very righteousness of God. This is the beautiful new image and identity that is ours in Christ. I call it an extreme makeover!

Jesus had His identity made like ours so we could now have His identity. In the bread we remember how He is like us in every physical and soulish way. When you come to Him in prayer He understands and knows whatever physical pains you are going through, He has gone through all of it. And when we come to Him with great emotional torment, feeling rejection, betrayal, abandonment, mockery and not fitting in, remember Jesus came to His own people, and was not received. And even when you confess/admit your sins to Him, He doesn't stand there with a condemning look in His eyes; you will see understanding and acceptance because He became sin. Now Jesus is our perfect High Priest because He became sin, sin on any level. Yes He can meet us and cover our gossip, our porn, our lies, our stealing, (there are so many ways to steal today) our addictive behaviors and abusive ways, any thing we are ashamed of or feel guilty about even murder.

Blood has always been special to God! It is life to us, we can live without most of our body parts, but blood is life to our bodies. It was the blood of an animal used as a sin offering in the Old Covenant that satisfied God's requirements. The writer of the Hebrews said, "without the shedding of blood there is no forgiveness of sins" (Hebrews 9:22). So when Jesus lifted up the cup, be it the wine or grape juice He was referring to His life, His life would soon be flowing from His brow while He hung on that cross (1 Peter 2:24). It is the blood that cleanses us of our sins and gives us a clean conscience so we can live freely.

From the outside looking in at the Church I am sure people have seen our obsession with the blood as barbaric, but what people need to think about is the holiness of God. We need to encourage people to see that because God is holy, He has to punish sin. But, God in His grace, mercy and justice was able to satisfy His holy requirements through Jesus' blood shed on the cross. Some of the best songs ever written are centered in the blood of Christ and explain this truth better than I ever could. For example:

THE OLD RUGGED CROSS
Vs. 3
George Bennard
In that old rugged cross, so despised by the world,
Has a wondrous attraction for me;
For the dear Lamb of God left His glory above
To bear it above to dark Calvary

WHEN I SURVEY THE WONDROUS CROSS
Vs. 3
Isaac Watts
See, from His head, His hands, His feet,
Sorrow and love flow mingled down:
Did e'er such love and sorrow meet?
Or thorns compose so rich a crown?

ARE YOU WASHED IN THE BLOOD?
Vs. 1
Elisha A. Hoffman

Have you been to Jesus for the cleansing power?
Are you washed in the blood of the Lamb?
Are you fully trusting in His grace this hour?
Are you washed in the blood of the Lamb?
Are you washed in the blood?
In the soul-cleansing blood of the Lamb?

AND CAN IT BE THAT I SHOULD GAIN?
Vs. 1
Charles Wesley

And can it be that I should gain an interest in the Savior's blood?
Died He for me, who caused Him pain? For me,
Who Him to death pursued? Amazing love!
How can it be that Thou my God shouldst die for me?

Throughout history people have stumbled about and have been tripped up by this issue of the blood. When I was a youth Pastor I had a very unusual experience one Communion Sunday. Michael was one of my youth group kids; he found his identity in Communion in a rather unusual way. Michael was a teen looking for acceptance, he had a birth defect and his ears came out from his head. I must admit but never said that he reminded me of Dumbo the elephant who had a self image problem, but what he was laughed at for, would become a saving thing as those ears would allow him to fly. Imagine an elephant flying. Well, it was hard to look at Michael and not focus on his ears. Michael not only had self image problems, but I knew he was disillusioned since his dad, who was his hero, had an affair and left the home. Even though Michael had these problems in his life, he did have a lot going for him. I knew his heart and that He loved the Lord Jesus, He knew his Bible well, and had many great stories of faith put to memory. At his core he was an inspiring person. But, because of his negative identity, he was always doing outlandish things to draw attention to himself.

At our church we celebrated the Lord's Supper on a monthly basis. I don't know if Michael premeditated his not so glorious Lord's Supper or not. But when the bread wafers were passed, Michael who was sitting in the second row took the wafer and ground in up into granules and then snorted it up his nose, like you see Hollywood movie stars snorting cocaine. Well, the little old ladies sitting across from him about lost their false teeth and their wigs, they were aghast. Michael took the cup of grape juice in a respectful way. Immediately after this "Memorial" service, these ladies dashed to me and in disgust told me about Michael's behavior. I would meet with Michael as a friend and as a Pastor.

And now, the rest of the story: I asked Michael without condemnation, "Hey, Michael, is snorting a communion wafer up your nose what you think Jesus meant when He said: Do this in remembrance of me?" He said no, and then we talked about what was really going on in his life, and his true identity in Jesus. I reminded him that behavior always flows out of identity. And with tears I am happy to tell you that Michael expressed godly sorrow for his actions, he apologized to the people who were offended. Michael went on to became a great student leader, a real worshipper, a joyous young man who began to live his covenant and communion identity. He became a very positive example for the younger kids in the group and today he is a very good preacher. Michael is a man of God, a man who loves God with all his heart, and a powerful communicator of the Word of God. I often think about what if I would have approached Michael from a condemnation standpoint and not from an identity standpoint, he might have run in rebellion. But because the Lord encouraged me to focus on his Covenant Identity, Michael is now another man who loves that OLD RUGGED CROSS, and lives like a rock with security from identity theft.

Section Four:
ROCK IT!

The wise man built his house upon the rock.
Matthew 7:25

They all ate the same spiritual food and drank the same spiritual drink; for they drank from the spiritual rock that accompanied them, and that rock was Christ.
I Corinthians 10:4

On this rock I will build my church.
Matthew 16:18

From the computer world we will use the word **"Authorization"** to understand what it means to "rock" our identity. Authorization is the action of giving someone permission to have something, or to do something.

Today in computer systems security engineers have made the process of authorization an important last step in the sequencing in the control access process. In this final step before access is granted and the user then has permission to enter the computer system or network the system administrator makes an evaluation based on the previous authentication and the encrypted information on their card. The authorization process is used to decide if user X is allowed to have access to data certain functionality or if this user will be denied access and given no access or limited to service Y. For example how much storage space will this user be given? Or how many hours of service will this user be granted? Or what files and directories will this user be able to access. In reality this authorization process is the step where various permissions are granted.

In this phase of access control the system administrator defines for the system the levels of authority this user is to have. For example, will this user be given permission to access individual files? Items data? Computer programs? Computer devices? Or other networks? All of these levels of authorization are administered to provide this system or corporation with security.

From a spiritual standpoint our mind is our system administrator and we must to train it to deny access to deny access to evil influences. We need to determine what thoughts we are to give authorizations to. And what levels of access we are going to give to certain sensual thoughts, greedy thoughts, revenge thoughts, or proud thoughts. Unless we control the access into our minds we can give the Identity Thief permission to have entrance into our hearts and the opportunity to do us harm.

The Apostle Paul understood this process of authorization and he encouraged believers in Jesus to, "Finally, brothers, whatever is true, whatever is noble, whatever is right, whatever is pure, whatever is lovely, whatever is admirable—if anything is excellent or praiseworthy—think about such things" (Philippians 4:8).

He is asking us to control the access to our hearts by only authorizing the thoughts to enter our minds and hearts that are consistent with our true identity in Jesus.

Constant awareness of wearing the CROWN (Christ, Righteousness, Order, Worship, and Nobility) is a powerfully positive way to exercise the "control access" security steps that will help us live with security from identity theft.

The acrostic CROWN is a way believers in Jesus can know that we are Authenticated, Encrypted, and Authorized. We are now able to live out of our true identity in Jesus Christ, and use this grid to prevent unauthorized entrance. We should use this grid to tell the Identity Thief that his access is denied! And then use this grid to say thank you to God for by faith in Jesus our access is accepted and we now have security from identity theft.

Something to think about: How can we use our access to God, and our authorization to help others enter the kingdom. Think about the "keys" we have been given to the kingdom (Matthew 16:19).

Chapter 14
THE ATTRIBUTES OF GOD "ROCK" OUR IDENTITY

Psalm 18:2-3

The LORD is my rock, my fortress and my deliverer;
My God is my rock, in whom I take refuge.
He is my shield and the horn of my salvation,
My stronghold. I call to the LORD, who is worthy of praise.

We are made in the image of God and we were specially made to know God! But, do we really know what God is like? A study of the attributes of God will help us know Him better so we can more excellently worship Him. Getting to know God's attributes helps us learn to rely upon Him as our rock, which is what He wants. He wants us to be like the wise man who built his life on the Rock (Matt. 7:24).

No one buys a new car and then just stores it in the garage. No, for goodness sake, we get out on the road and we drive. We plan excursions just so we can be in our new car and see what it can do. We get out the owners manual and we check out all the cool stuff that comes with our car. We get all excited because we keep finding new stuff to try out and we feel great about our ride when we find that so much comes as standard equipment.

Can you imagine a new believer, only checking God out on Sunday mornings? Or just looking to other people to see all that God is about? No, God is the most awesome being in the universe and we get to know Him personally, He is infinite, but makes Himself intimate with us. We will never be bored searching out the awesome things of God, and getting to Know the attributes of God is a powerful way to "Rock", secure, fortify, and substantiate our faith in Him.

I have never been involved with a new school that is trying to establish their identity and are creating their team's mascot. I come from Nebraska and I have to tell you that "Herby Husker" the inflatable and loveable oversized farmer in the red and white striped overalls doesn't strike fear in anyone. Usually teams try to come up with a fierce identity that intimidates their opponents, like a Viking, or a bear, even a hurricane, but I have seen a school with a lamb as a mascot. They called themselves the Lambkins. That has got to be the wimpiest mascot of all. My point is simple, we get to choose our identity and we ought to choose God as our model. His character and personality are the most noble to admire. Ephesians 5:1 says, "Be imitators of God."

Sadly, most people do not look to God to establish their identity, they do just the opposite, and they try to make God into their own image. They make God into their preferences, political, music, culture, and personality. If someone is really into liberal or conservative politics, often their view of God will follow this bent. Even when it comes to culture, we have a tendency to picture God being even our skin color, or our ethnic background. I don't mean to freak you out with these thoughts, but for the next few minutes, don't put God into your box, take a good look at His attributes, His characteristics and see what He is like, and then let these great traits impact your identity.

As we take a look at His attributes, be thinking about how His characteristics can influence our, mind, our heart, our conscience and morality. The apostle Paul wrote to the Romans, "For although they knew God, they neither glorified His as God nor gave thanks to Him, but their thinking became futile and their foolish hearts were darkened. Although they claimed to be wise, they became fools and exchanged the glory of the immortal God for images made to look like mortal man and birds and animals and reptiles. Therefore God gave them over in the sinful desires of their hearts to sexual impurity for the degrading of their bodies with one another. They exchanged the truth of God for a lie, and worshipped and served created things rather than the creator—who is forever praised. Amen" (Romans 1:20-25).

This study of the attributes of God is designed to help us get a glimpse of God so we can know how glorious He is. The natural response to this study will be praise to God; we will begin to lose ourselves in His awesomeness. When we lose ourselves in Him this is when our identity becomes transformed into His identity. We were made in His image, and studying these attributes gives the Holy Spirit latitude to move us into His grand design.

At first we will be overwhelmed by His moral attribute of Holiness, Love and Justice. And we will be challenged to learn to rely on His non-moral attributes of sovereignty, eternality, omniscience, omnipresence, omnipotence, and you will be thankful He is immutable (He changes not).

THE MORAL ATTRIBUTES OF GOD:
Righteousness / Holiness
Justice
Love
Truth

Righteousness/ Holiness: This means it is impossible for God to Sin

INSIGHT: Even though we know that God is love, Just, and True, we start this study with Righteousness/Holiness because this is the dominate characteristic of God. We never read in the Bible God is: Truth, truth, truth, of Just, Just, Just, or Love, Love, Love, but we have heard Isaiah say, "Holy, Holy, Holy is the Lord Almighty; the whole earth is full of His glory" (Isaiah 6:3).

This attribute convicts us in our core because the writer of the book of Hebrews said, "Make every effort to live in peace with all men and to be holy; without holiness no one will see the Lord" (Hebrews 12:14).

We rejoice in the Gospel of Jesus because by believing in the Gospel, unholy people become holy by faith (See, Romans 5:1). Paul said, "For in the gospel a righteousness from God is revealed, a righteousness that is by faith, from first to last, just as it is written: the righteous will live by faith" (Romans 1:17).

APPLICATION OF THIS ATTRIBUTE:
Worship God in Holiness
Submit ourselves to the process of sanctification
We learn to hate sin, and desire to hate sin because of how sin affects our relationship with God and others (1 Thessalonians 4:1-4).

Justice: This means it is impossible for God to do anything unjust.

INSIGHT: Paul, Silas and Timothy wrote to the church of the Thessalonians and reminded them of the justice of God by saying, "All this is evidence that God's judgment is right, and as a result you will be counted worthy of the Kingdom of God, for which you are suffering. God is just: He will pay back trouble to those who trouble you and give relief to you who are troubled, and to us as well" (2 Thessalonians. 1:5-6).

APPLICATION OF THIS ATTRIBUTE:
　　Rest in God and trust Him to make things right. Vengeance belongs to God (Romans 12:9-21).
　　If you are living rightly, be comforted. And if your life is not consistent with God's justice, consider yourself warned. To live in an unjust way is not consistent with our identity in God who is Just.

Love: This means God always brings out His highest and best good. This truth secures the believer, and draws the unbeliever to Him.

INSIGHTS: I John 4:7-8 says, "Dear Friends, let us love one another, for love comes from God. Everyone who loves has been born of God and knows God. Whoever does not love does not know God, because God is love. This is how God showed His love among us; He sent His one and only Son into the world that we might live through Him."

APPLICATION OF THIS ATTRIBUTE:
　　We can always rely on God to love us. As we grow in faith and believe more confidently in the love of God we become more secure.

We can learn to live above the fears of life because His perfect love, "casts out our fears" (I John 4:18). We can walk confidently with God, knowing that nothing can separate us from the love of God (Romans 8:35-39).

Truth: This means that God is not a man that He can lie (Numbers 23:19). His Word is truth (John 17:17), and His truth is what sets people free (John 8:32). Jesus said He was the truth (John 14:6).

INSIGHTS: Don't fight the truth, learn it and love it and rely upon it. I call it "Mt. Truth" and it is the rock solid bank to Grace River. It will never move, and we can lean into it all our lives. It is the reliable guide and boundary to life in Grace River. God's Word, the Ten Commandments, the New Covenant and truth in science and history should be our best friends.[14]

APPLICATION OF THIS ATTRIBUTE: Learn to lean into Mt. Truth, when confronted with a difficult situation always ask, "what is the truth." And learn to look for a scripture, a precept, or a principle to rely upon.

THE NON-MORAL ATTRIBUTES OF GOD:
The expressed and awesome characteristics that only God possesses. No other being has these abilities.

Eternality
Sovereignty
Immutability
Omniscience
Omnipotence

The Eternality of God: This means God created time and is in control of time. He is not bound by time or limited by time in any way.

---

[14] See Appendix #2, p. 220, The Grace River Model.

INSIGHTS: With God time is quantum, and this means He sees all time, past, present and future as now! Therefore, God is without end, and in Him believers Have life eternal.

APPLICATION: God has an eternal perspective and we need to learn to look at our situations from this eternal perspective. He set eternity in our hearts; therefore we can learn to live for eternity and not just the pressure of the urgent. He always knows in advance how He will bring things together. This means we can learn to trust him, wait patiently for Him, and rest in Him because He is never hurried, and yet always on time, His time. Therefore we can, "Be still and wait on the Lord" (Psalm 46:10).

Key Scripture, "Now to the King Eternal, immortal, invisible, the only God, be honor and glory forever and ever Amen" (1 Tim. 1:17).

The **Sovereignty** of God: God is the creator and ruler of the universe, He is supreme and He is in control, He is the King of His Kingdom.

Key Scripture, "The LORD has established His throne in heaven, and His kingdom rules over all." Psalm 103:19.

INSIGHT: God causes all things to work together the way He wants them to, He even uses, Satan, sin and conflict to accomplish His ultimate purpose (Romans 8:28).

APPLICATION: He is my king, He is establishing His kingdom in my heart, because He is the Lord, I will let Him have the control and position He deserves. I will trust Him to work all things out for our good (Romans 8:28-29).

IDENTITY ISSUE: He is my King and He is Lord of my life (He owns me, rules me, and is ultimately responsible for me).

The **Immutability** of God: This means that God does not change, He does not mutate, he doesn't have to adapt to a changing world because He is perfect.

INSIGHT: Conformity to Jesus Christ is my aim, because trying to keep changing to meet the standards of this world is unrealistic (I John 2:15-16).

Key Scripture, "Jesus Christ is the same yesterday and today and forever" (Hebrews 13:8).

APPLICATION: God keeps His word, He is not like shifting sand, so I can always have a sure standing with Him. I am established on the Rock Christ Jesus and have security from identity theft.

IDENTITY ISSUE: Fads and fashions come and go, and so does the favor of people, because people are fickle, I will find my identity in God who is unchanging. If I were to try to please people I would have to be changing to adjust to them and their whims all the time. Because God is immutable I can become a steady and consistent person. Therefore I will quit worrying about what other people think of me, because what God thinks matters the most, and He will not change His feelings about me.

God is **Omniscient**: He knows everything about everything.

Key Scripture, "Can anyone hide in secret places so that I cannot see Him?" Declares the LORD. Do not I fill heaven and earth? Declares the LORD" (Jeremiah 23:24).

INSIGHT: There is no reason not to be real! I will live transparently with God and keep short accounts with Him.

APPLICATION: I should not even try to hide anything from God because He knows everything anyway. Therefore I will find freedom in my relationship with Him by being, open, honest and transparent. I will quickly confess my sins, and enjoy the benefits of God being merciful and gracious towards me (Isaiah 66:1-2, I John 1:9).

IDENTITY ISSUE: I will live with God as my audience, lay everything bare before Him, and not try to fake Him or others out about my life. I do not have to be a fake.

The **Omnipresence** of God: God is everywhere present at the same time. There is no where He is not!

INSIGHT: Because God is everywhere, no matter where I am, He is there to support me with His love, wisdom and presence. No matter where I am, I am in God's presence and in His presence is fullness of Joy, therefore I can always be joyful (Psalms 16:11).

Key Scripture, "Be strong and courageous. Do not be afraid or terrified because of them, for the LORD your God goes with you; He will never leave you nor forsake you" (Deuteronomy 31:6).

INSIGHT: No matter where I am, God is there.

APPLICATION: Where ever I am, I will practice the presence of God. And even though there are lots of other eyes watching me, I only care about His, the other eyes are not so intimidating.

IDENTITY ISSUE: God is where ever I am therefore I can always be secure, and full of Joy. The Joy of the Lord is my strength (Nehemiah. 8:10). I will concentrate on living for this wonderful audience of one, God. I will be aware of my tendency to try to draw identity significance from the "6 P's", and when I am convicted of this I will quickly be reminded of the Lord's presence and find comfort and identity in Him alone.

The **Omnipotence** of God: God is all powerful; He made the world and the universe merely by speaking them into existence.

Key Scriptures, "Great is our Lord mighty in power; His

understanding has no limit" (Psalm 147:5).

"But our citizenship is in heaven, and we eagerly await a savior from there, the Lord Jesus Christ, who by the power that enables Him to bring everything under His control, will transform our lowly bodies so that they will be like His glorious body" (Phil. 3:20-21).

INSIGHT: God is able to change my life, nothing limits His ability, by faith I will join Him in His glorious plan.

APPLICATION: It is not my strength and creative abilities I rely upon, my strength is in the Lord. "I can do everything through Him who gives me strength" (Phil 4:13). He can change me, my circumstances and even the world around me, so I will trust in His strength and not try to do everything my self. Just like it is easier to take a lug nut off of a wheel with a tire iron, and not my fingers, I will learn to rely on His glorious strength.

IDENTITY ISSUE: It is not my physical muscles that are the most important; I will build my spiritual muscles so I can rely on God's strength. My strength is limited, His is omnipotent.

I have found that there are few disciplines that can "rock" our identity in God like meditating on these attributes. Let me suggest that you take one of these attributes per day and practice praising Him for that particular attribute (Take a three by five note card, and write out your Attribute of God for the day, then list the key scripture, the insight, your application and your identity issue you are trusting Him for. Carry this card with you and watch God become bigger to you as you get to know Him better by getting to know Him in His attributes.). When we lose ourselves in these awesome characteristics of God, our lives will be substantiated in Him and we will begin to believe that we truly have security from identity theft.

Chapter 15
GOD'S PURPOSES FOR HIS LAWS
Exodus 20, Psalm 34:5, Galatians 2-3

David was one of my all-time favorite students, he really was, I am not just putting a spin on this story I am about to tell. As a junior in high school, David was in my Bible class, he was an engaging student who loved to discuss the Bible and relate God's Word to the issues of the day. You could always count on David for a laugh, or an insightful comment. We studied the book of Romans and were learning how to live as a Christ follower without acting religious. We enjoyed many sessions where our classroom was transformed into a sanctuary and we experienced God in a special way. We came to believe that when you open the Word of God, face the truth and embrace grace by faith we knew we were meeting the living God.

I remember a day when David was so overwhelmed with his own sin that while attending the required chapel service where a visiting evangelist brought a message that the Holy Spirit used to tackle David's heart. I was privileged to join this evangelist and pray sincere and contrite prayers with David after this service. We were all confident that God was doing a transforming work in David, and David wasn't shy about his desire to change his ways and begin to trust and obey.

The Identity Thief was attacking David on many fronts. David is a Korean young man who had been adopted into a loving and authentic Christian family. In my opinion his parents couldn't have loved and cared for him more, they seemed to know how to bring the best out of David, and provided him with every opportunity to grow. David was loaded with athletic ability and his parents sacrificed to make sure David could attend the camps, clinics and have the coaching to become the fine all-conference and All-State soccer player he became. It was a family affair and David's brothers and sister all played the game and enjoyed all aspects of athletic competition. It was heart warming to see this family live the life and throw themselves into this season and share this soccer adventure together.

David was not only a gifted athlete, he was a fierce competitor. He was one of those players who made everyone on his team better. He was exceptionally fast and could dribble around his opponent, or pass to a team mate. In one way or another he was always attacking the goal, or stuffing the other teams attempts at goal. He helped his team win the Colorado State High School Championship title. All the while he was competing in sports he was battling many identity battles. David had a beautiful white girl friend, yet because of his race he was forbidden to pursue this relationship. David and I talked and dealt with the pain this prejudice aroused in him.

David was experiencing another form of Identity Theft in the physical area of his life. During a soccer game he took a hard kicked soccer ball as a shot to his head, and he lost some of the vision in his right eye, and now he could no longer see the ball at his feet on that one side. His identity was being threatened because David was only seeing himself as a soccer player. Simply put, that was his identity, and now that his soccer abilities were being diminished, he felt diminished as a person too.

In our Bible class we were learning how salvation was based on our relationship with Jesus Christ alone and not based on law or rule keeping. David was severely conflicted with this truth because at every turn in his life he was being bound up and confronted by rules and regulations. It seemed as if the school's student hand book had become as thick as a phone book, and every freedom he wanted was nixed by a litany of rules. David by nature is a fun loving and out going person but every fun and expressive thing he wanted to do was squashed by the schools rules and the sad faced enforcers. This was starting to mess with his mind because in sincerity David also loved God and everyone else and wanted to be a respectful person, but this restrictive environment wasn't consistent with the freedom David was reading about in his Bible.

Like most high school students David had a very sensitive "radar detector" that beeped loud and often at the sightings of hypocrisy. And when he witnessed parents, coaches, administrators, teachers, and even church leaders acting inconsistent with what was being preached or with the scriptures, David struggled to fight off disillusionment. He asked provocative questions in class, like, is this Christian life worth the effort? I remember having lively and engaging discussions in class where David enthusiastically voiced his opinions and his feelings about this hypocrisy. He had heard about the laws of God from a dos and don'ts stand point, and so many of the school rules didn't make sense to him. We tried to talk about the letter of the law verses the spirit of the law. We talked about loving God and living with God as our audience and not focusing on other people. We discussed a religious attitude toward rules, and we negated the licentious and rebellious attitudes that are so prevalent in our society and churches today. I encouraged David and his classmates to get to know the scriptures and find the true freedom Jesus purchased for us with His blood and then live in it respectfully in the power of the Holy Spirit.

My students were candid with me and talked about how all they wanted to do was get out of school and go on a sinning spree. They talked about how they wanted to get tattoos, piercings, get drunk, have sex, and even vandalize. We discussed this response to the grace of God and I let them know that this just showed a lack of understanding of God's grace towards them. I encouraged them to live a respectful thank you life for God, but they wanted to rebel. I tried to get them to see that if they really knew how much God loved them, they would naturally love Him in such a way that it would really hurt them to sin against Him.

It became clear to me that these students had the law laid down on them without being brought in to relationship with God and their leaders. Josh McDowell, a famous Christian apologist, used to say, "rules without relationship leads to rebellion." This was proving to be the case with these students. David might have known intellectually how God loved him and that His laws were given for many positive reasons. I wish we would have taken the time to assimilate how God's Ten Commandments were given to Protect us, Provide us with blessing, and to Prompt us to come to know Jesus (Galatians 3:24), and to help us personalize our identity in Him.

We have all heard the story about the grade school student who was disciplined by his teacher and forced to sit on a chair in the corner of the room, a time out experience away from the other students. Another teacher walked in and commented to this student about how he was sitting so nice and being polite. The student then responded, "I might be sitting down on the outside but I am standing up on the inside." This illustrates how these high school students were, they were keeping the rules extrinsically, but in their hearts and minds they wanted to rebel in a big way. They were giving lip service to God and this institution but in reality their hearts were far away. This school had a reputation for seeing its graduates go off the deep end; there were stories of rebellion after graduation that resulted in pregnancies, vandalism, drug use, and wild living. It took me becoming an insider to understand what was going on that predicated these behaviors.

David was in the same situation; he was fed up with playing the religious rule keeping game, but he held on to stay eligible to play soccer. He hadn't personalized what Jesus said in John 14:21, "Whoever has my commands and obeys them, he is the one who loves me. He who loves me will be loved by my Father, and I too will love him and show myself to him." He hadn't learned in his heart the value of heart felt motivation of loving God intrinsically. All he had experienced was a forced extrinsic "have to" religious type of performance based way of acting. And because he didn't want to be the hypocrite (play-actor), he thought oh, what the heck, I will just be true to my self and rebel. I passionately wanted David and all my students to personally know how good life could be for them when Jesus shows Himself to them as a result of them yielding to Him and obeying Him with their hearts.

After David graduated from high school he went to a college in Iowa where he could play out his identity as a soccer player with a scholarship. It was more than a year since I had last seen David, but when I went to the University of Northern Colorado to visit my children for a parent's weekend, I saw him at a tailgate party. He was sloshing around drunk, holding a bottle of beer in his hand calling out Mr. Huston, Mr. Huston. I remember hugging David, but our conversation wasn't coherent, nor was David's identity. He wasn't living out of his true identity as a blood bought and dearly loved child of God. His college years were a dangerous time for David. He drove fast cars and a motorcycle, chased skirts and tried to be known as the party guy. To David's credit he worked hard and developed himself as a salesman and from a worldly standpoint he is set to score the big bucks.

This story of David can be told a thousand times over. We all know of terrific young people who go off to college and leave their faith and morals in their high school locker. I believe this happens because these students were never given the freedom to own their own faith and encouraged to seek and find their true identity in Jesus. They were force-fed the laws of God and were not allowed to see the grace of God in His laws and commandments. And when the laws of God were taught they were transmitted in such a dogmatic way that they never got in on the love and relational side of the negative commandments. The "Thou shalt nots" of the Ten Commandments can come off as negative and restrictive to a teenager or an adult for that matter. But, it doesn't take much to communicate all of the positive reasons behind these negative commands. I have already mentioned that they were given to protect, provide, prompt and to help us personalize our identity in God. But, preachers, teachers and even parents have a tendency of laying down the law and failing to show us the Father's heart and the benefits hidden in His commands, and laws.

God's Children, Israel had a history of abandoning God in a similar way. Even though God constantly reminded them about His faithfulness, and care for them they were prone to wonder from Him. When God gave His Ten Commandments He prefaced these famous ten commands by stating that He was the LORD their God who brought them out of Egypt, and out of slavery. This is an appeal to His grace, and a positive way to set up these commands that are intended to secure His children in His love.

God knew that the Identity Thief would be constantly attacking them so in Exodus 19:5 He said to them, "Now if you obey me fully and keep my covenant, then out of all nations you will be my treasured possession. Although the whole earth is mine, you will be for me a kingdom of priests and a Holy Nation." It was Moses who relayed these identity enriching words from the heart of God to the people. And they indicated that they had the resolve to do everything the

LORD had said (Ex: 19:8). But we know that the human spirit is willing but the flesh is weak. And even the Apostle Paul would confess in Romans 7:18: for I have the desire to do good, but I cannot carry it out." He also said: I do not understand what I do. For what I want to do, I do not do, but what I hate I do" (7:15). He would go on to explain that the laws of God themselves are powerless to change our lives as we have been weakened by our own sinful nature. So we must reckon that even though the laws of God are a wonderful gift from God without the Spirit of God, and without learning how to walk in the power of the Holy Spirit the laws, rules and commandments can make us more miserable.

Think of it, even though the laws are wonderful protective boundaries, and foundational pillars for our civilization, without the Spirit of God guiding us and empowering us, these very laws can bury our human spirit under guilt, shame and condemnation. They do this because they constantly remind us about how we are not measuring up to them, and the more we try to keep them in our own efforts the more we feel the sting of failure. But, when we believe the good news about the blood of Jesus, and are born again by the Holy Spirit making us alive in God, we can be delivered from this condemnation (Romans 8:1-3). The Spirit led person can learn to appreciate the convicting work of the Holy Spirit in our hearts who communicates to us that He is with us, for us, and working in us to make us more like Jesus. He also puts with in us the desire to keep God's commandments so we can have His provision, protection and enjoy the sense of His pleasure.

Once we understand the role the Holy Spirit plays in transforming our lives, and aligning our lives according to God's Word (John 17:17), the more we can relax in Him and trust Him. God had taken Moses on a camp out to help him understand His purposes for His laws. Prior to the giving of the Law on Mt. Sinai God reminded them that they were "Passover People, and how He had brought them out of Egypt on Eagles Wings. I believe this was a picture of the Spirit filled life. He constantly reassures them of their identity by reminding them who they are in Him. He calls them a kingdom of Priests, a Holy Nation, and tells them again and again that they are precious to Him (Exodus 19).

In Exodus Chapter 20 God gives to Moses and all mankind the gift of His Ten Commands, He says: 'You shall have no other gods before me. "You shall not make for yourself an idol in the form of anything in heaven above or on the earth beneath or in the waters below. You shall not bow down to them or worship them; for I the LORD your God, am a jealous God, punishing the children for the sin of the fathers to the third and forth generation of those who hate me, but showing love to a thousand (generations). of those who love me and keep my commandments. "You shall not misuse the name of the LORD your God, for the LORD will not hold anyone guiltless who misuses His name. Remember the Sabbath day by keeping it holy. Six days you shall labor and do all your work, but the seventh day is a Sabbath to the LORD your God. On it you shall not do any work, neither you, nor your son or daughter, nor your manservant or maidservant, nor your animals, nor the alien within your gates. For in six days the LORD made the heavens and the earth, the sea and all that is in them, but He rested on the seventh day. Therefore the LORD blessed the Sabbath day and made it holy. "Honor your father and mother, so that you may live long in the land the LORD your God is giving you. You shall not murder. You shall not commit adultery. You shall not steal. "You shall not give false testimony against your neighbor. You shall not covet your neighbor's house. You shall not covet your neighbor's wife, or his manservant or maidservant, his ox or donkey, or anything that belongs to your neighbor" (Ex. 20:1-18).

These landmark laws are all about our identity and our relationships with God and others. Sadly most of the people in our world can only list a couple of these commandments, and fewer yet have been taught about grace of God in them, and fewer yet have ever taken a look at how God shows us His identity and our identity in these precious Ten Commandments. In these bedrock commandments our identity in God finds a sure foundation to build upon. These great commands were given to impart to us God's identity and to make us like a Rock!

God introduces these ten commands by reminding us of who He is and the relationship He wants with us. We see His heart for us, and we are reminded that He heard the cries of His children and delivered them from bondage in Israel and was leading them into His promised land so that they could enjoy life together. His chief aim is to have a relationship with us, so we can enjoy Him. David, and all of us need to be reminded of how God desires relationship and the primary purpose of His laws is to help us enter into identity and relationship with Him by seeing Him in His laws.

In Verse three we are told to not have other Gods. God is using this command to remind us not to try to find any other identity outside of Him. And in Ephesians 5:1, the Apostle Paul tells us to be imitators of God. This first command proves to be the foundation of our identity and our relationship with God; it gives our lives true meaning and value. I Verse four we are told by God not to have any idols. God wants us to avoid pursuing the "Ps" the Identity Thief uses to rob us of our true significance. These Ps include our Possessions, Physical appearance, Power, Prestige, Performance and Position. All of these can be idols that distract us from worshipping God in Spirit and truth. These Ps are fleshly ways we are tempted to meet our own needs in our own ways, God wants us to learn to go to Him and trust Him to meet our needs, so he says no idols.

God makes His Identity emphasis clear in these commands when in Verse seven He tells us to take care of His name. When we truly value and lift up His name we are reverent and worshipful. This is to be what we are known for, this is our identity. And just as children take their fathers name, we are privileged to be blessed with our Heavenly Fathers name, and character. This is what sets us apart; there is no better identity, for in this identity goodness and mercy follow us all the days of our lives (Psalm 23). He then tells us in Verse 8 to keep the Sabbath holy; God set the example here by working the six days of creation and then resting from His work on the seventh. By doing this he set a rhythm for us, and built rest into our lives as a quality that is to mark our identity. Jesus said, "The Sabbath was made for man, not man for the Sabbath" (Mark 2:27). This provision lifts up our value to God, and imparts to us an identity as Sabbath keeping people, people who find their rest, provision and peace in God (Phil 4:6-7).

In Verse twelve God gives us a commandment that has a huge promise attached to it, the promise of an abundant and long life. He tells us to honor our parents, this attitude and disposition not only looks good on us it is our identity. We are to be known as people of honor. The other day while standing in line at Wal-Mart I had to tolerate children disrespecting their parents, what an ugly experience this was. I thought about how their behavior was flowing out of their sense of identity. These children obviously hadn't been taught this command, and then I was struck with how our Heavenly Father imparts this command to us by modeling it, and graciously asking for honor in return (Ephesians 6:1).

The first four commands focuses on our relationship with God, and the next six focus on our relationships with others. He started with an admonition to honor our parents, and then He puts simple and straight forward commands to us that communicate clear values and if we look close we can see our identity because these laws are like looking in a mirror (James 1:23). He concisely tells us not to murder. In saying this He imparts to us an identity of life, people who value life and are life-giving. Even though we walk in the valleys and in the shadows of death, we are known for being "life" to a dying world. We have seen this by all the Christian missions, hospitals, orphanages, and care giving ministries God's children bring to the world. This is who we are; we are life to the world. Jesus said, "I am the way, the truth, and the life" (John 14:6).

In verse fourteen He clearly states that we are not to commit adultery. He is telling us that we are to be people who have fidelity unto Him and our families. Having been a Pastor for over twenty five years I have witnessed many lives being destroyed by indiscretions and infidelity. The people who think its my life and my body and what I do with my sexual desires only affects me do not understand why God said "no adultery". In saying no adultery God is telling us that we are people who put righteousness above personal pleasure. We are to be known for being chaste, self-controlled and people who build relationships and who don't tear them down. Jesus expanded upon this issue when He implied that our true identity in God even impacts how we care for our hearts and take discipline over our minds and our eyes.

He tells us that adultery starts with a lack of understanding about our true identity. Jesus said in Matthew 5:28, "But I tell you that anyone who looks at a woman lustfully has already committed adultery with her in his heart."

I learn so much from God about communications, and in verse fifteen he assumes nothing when He says no stealing. You might think this could go without saying, but God wants it in writing for the entire world to know that we are people who respect others and we have a high view of justice. Stealing is not consistent with our true identity in God, for we believe that he can meet all our needs. So we learn to work and wait on Him. By finding this kind of contentment in God we come to the blessed place where we realize that we, "can do everything through Him who gives us strength" (Phil. 4:13). Jesus told a story about a man who wanted bigger and bigger barns for all of his stuff, but he died before he could enjoy it because he wasn't rich in God (Luke 12:18). Because we find our identity in God we can be truly rich in Him, and find true pleasure in Him, this is what we are to be known for.

Truth is so important to God that he makes it the ninth command by saying "no lies, no falsehood!" John captures this thought when he calls us children of light. So with us there is not to be deception, shadows or dark lies. We are to be transparent people who even expose the deeds of darkness (Ephesians 5:11). We are people who live anchored into the truth, and set free by knowing and living truthfully (John 8:32). He concludes these famous commands with a similar thought, No coveting! To covet would mean that we have our minds and hearts divided on all sorts of things that are not ours. Just as God began these Ten Commands with the first command to have no other God's, He concludes these Ten by telling us that we are single minded. Our identity in found in Him alone, and we are to keep our eyes fixed on Him and thankful for His provision. To be looking around at another persons house or wife is not consistent with who we are. What He is saying to us is my children have their minds fixed on me and on heaven (Col. 3:1, Matt. 6:10). We are people who don't live for this worlds stuff, we are holy and devoted people who are heavenly minded because our true rewards are not of this world, the command to not covet sits well with us, because we are focused on Him.

After the giving of these Laws in Exodus 20 God continues to substantiate our identity in His Laws by taking the next several chapters of scripture to outline the Moral, Civil, Ceremonial, and Criminal laws. These laws have been foundational for life here on earth, and they are like the building blocks that become the pillars of our own identity. His Moral laws show us that we are Holy people in Him. His Civil Laws are to inspire us to see ourselves as respect based people. His Ceremonial Laws impress us to be humble and reverent people. And His Criminal Laws urge us to see ourselves as law-based and disciplined people. God has always identified people in accordance to His laws. He views the wicked as Lawless people, and His people who have been given these precious laws are considered as the righteous and law keeping people. The Psalmist of 119:97 would say, "I love thy Law!, I meditate on it all day long." This wise person knew that hidden in God's laws is His wisdom and our identity. No wonder we are encouraged to meditate on God's laws day and night! (Joshua 1:8, Psalm 1).

It wasn't long before God's children were disrespecting Him and His laws when God summoned Moses to come up the mountain. And God gave Moses tablets of stone with these laws and instructions inscribed upon them. The glory of the Lord Settled on Mount Sinai at this time and the cloud covered it for six days. On the seventh day God called out to Moses and Moses entered that cloud. And for forty days and nights Moses was on that mountain fellowshipping with God. At this time God asked Moses to go back to His people and collect gold, silver, blue, purple and scarlet linen, goats hair and ram skins, goat skins and wood and oil for lamps and special stones to make a tabernacle a mobile sanctuary for God to travel with His people. He wanted to dwell in their midst, and His laws were given to facilitate this, and His Tablets were to be a center piece on a mercy seat made of pure gold on top of the ark. God said that there He will meet with Moses and the people of Israel. This was to be a consecrated tent of meeting so that His people will know who He is and who they are in Him.

While this conversation was going on, down at the camp Aaron and the people were corrupting themselves by intentionally forgetting who they are as stated in God's commands. The Lord said to Moses, "Go down; for your people have corrupted themselves, turning quickly from the ways God had commanded them." They had collected Gold and silver alright, but they had assembled a golden calf and were behaving badly around this altar. It was is if they had graduated from a Christian High school and then went off to college and forget who they were.

We visually reflect upon the picture of Moses coming down the mountain with the gift of these tablets in his hands and seeing these people lathering themselves up in sin, his anger grew hot and he threw down these stone tables and they were broken at the foot of the mountain. He then took the golden calf and burnt it, ground it to a powder and made the people drink it. Moses then had to call the people to decide what there identity truly is, He asked, "who is on the Lord's side?" And the people who didn't identity with God fell by a plague the LORD sent.

God would once again show His grace to Moses and His people and had Moses cut two stone tablets and God replaced them writing His laws on these stone tablets. Moses confessed his sin and the sin of the people. He asked God to pardon and forgive them on the basis of His identity. When Moses came down off the mountain with these two tablets, his face was radiant because he had been talking with God. Moses had to put a veil on His face because the people were afraid to come near him.

The Apostle Paul would write about the importance of the law and our identity as radiant people in 2 Corinthians. 3:7-10: He said, "Now if the ministry that brought death, which was engraved in letters on stone came with glory, so that the Israelites could not look steadily at the face of Moses because of its glory, fading though it was, will not the ministry of the Spirit be even more glorious? If the ministry that condemns men is glorious, how much more glorious is the ministry that brings righteousness! For what was glorious has no glory now in comparison with the surpassing glory. And if what was fading away came with glory, how much greater is the glory of that which lasts!

Therefore since we have such a hope, we are very bold. We are not like Moses, who would put a veil over his face, to keep the Israelites from gazing at it while the radiance is fading away. But their minds were made dull, for to this day the same veil remains when the old covenant is read. It has not been removed, because only in Christ is it taken away. Even to this day when Moses is read, a veil covers their hearts. But whenever anyone turns to the Lord, the veil is taken away. Now the Lord is Spirit the Spirit and where the Spirit of the Lord is, there is Freedom."

God has great purposes for His laws. They protect us, provide for us many blessings, and they prompt us to come to Jesus by killing us (Gal. 3:24), and the help us personalize our identity in Jesus as we learn to believe and appropriate the power of the Holy Spirit. David like the children of Israel abandoned his faith and his morals while he went to college, but God is gracious towards Him and now his face is radiant because He is looking to God again and thanking Him for His grace that keeps on saving Him. He is learning the difference between condemnation and the caring convicting work the Holy Spirit does in our hearts to keep us in fellowship with God.

I know David can overcome the Identity Thief, by His faith in the blood of Christ, and constantly apply God's grace to his life. My prayer for David is Psalm 34:5, "Those who look to him are radiant; their faces are never covered in shame." I am trusting that David will come to the place where he can say with King David. "I love thy law." I know he will love it because he will know that it protects him, provides him with the blessings of God, and constantly prompts him to go to Jesus. Even today we should be quick to meditate on the Ten Commandments that God engraved in stone, and ask Him to help us see how these precious laws protect us, guard us with blessing, prompt us to come to now Jesus and help us personalize our identity in Him. We should know that there was a reason His laws were engraved in stone – to remind us that we are Like a Rock.

Chapter 16
GOD'S FEASTS

Psalm 122:1; Leviticus 23

When I started attending church out of my own volition I was in college and went with friends to the Kearney E-Free Church where I heard Pastor John McNeil open many of the morning services by saying King David's words, "I was glad when they said to me, let us go into the house of the LORD" (Psalm 122:1).

This famous text from Psalm 122 was confusing to me because prior to this time in my life I was never glad to go to church. I thought going to church was a waste of time, so strong was this conviction that I hid my basketball and basketball sneakers in the car, and would sneak out of church to practice, and would return to my family when the church bells rang again. I would fake like I had been in Church.

After I graduated from high school I had come to know Jesus and was now embarking on my journey of getting to know God, as now going to church was a glad thing for me. But, never in my wildest dreams did I imagine how good God intended for life to be in community with Him and His people. In the Old Testament book of Leviticus chapter 23 God instituted a number of perpetual feasts, also called festivals and Holy days as a way to impart His identity and a way to constantly remind us of who He is and how good it is to dwell together in unity with Him and each other.

God is the God of feasts; He is the loving Father in the famous parable of the Prodigal Son of Luke 15. In this parable we see a long faced son returning home to his father to be surprised by grace. The Father has been thinking about this son He loves and when he sees him in the distance he ran to greet him, embrace him and bless him with Gifts. He gave his son a robe, a ring, sandals and then he threw an extravagant party complete with Barbeque brisket sandwiches, to welcome him home. Such is the Love of the Father, our generous Heavenly Father God Almighty. He gave him gifts that reminded him of his true identity as a son, He gave him a robe to cover his shame and to remind him that he was a royal child. He gave him shoes for his feet to remind him that he wasn't a slave but he beloved son. And He gave him a ring to bless him again with His riches this ring would serve as a signet. Then he lavished him with a feast, this is how God is, He is one who likes to celebrate and He likes to celebrate in ways that imparts to us the message of our true identity. In this case, He wanted to celebrate to communicate to his son that he was lost but now he is found and safe with Him. And that he was once as good as dead but now he is home and alive and free. These are some of the great identity characteristics that come from being at home with Father.

David knew that God loved celebrating and feasting with His children and David knew of God's happiness when he said, "I was glad when they said to me let us go up to the house of the LORD." David knew that to party with God was one of the best things in life. The Bible lets us know of many reasons we who belong in God's family have to celebrate. We don't just TGIF, "thank God it is Friday! We know we can TGED, "thank God every day" because God has blessed every day that we get with Him (Romans 14:5). We don't need to put one day above another, yet as we look at the memorial and perpetual feasts that God has instituted in Leviticus 23 we can get a real identity boost from them because in them we learn about our heavenly Father and see how He has designed them to impart His identity characteristics to us.

Giving thanks to God was a foundational attitude in all these feasts and this created a very festive atmosphere. To add to the uplifting spiritual climate there was always events that reminded everyone of how faithful and generous God has been. There were games that filled the air with excitement, and the smells of great foods that invited everyone to the table. For some of these festivals it was like a week long camp meeting, with song fests, story telling and energetic dancing. You can see why a young guy would say "I was glad when they said let us go up to the house of the LORD." In the life of this great nation Israel there were lots of good things happening in this environment of worship and fellowship. Often a young guy would meet that special young lady, or his parents would eye the young lady for their young man. This was a joy filled environment of freedom, safety and a trusting community because this was a convocation God the Father had called them to and his boundaries made it the positive place to be. Even though God required attendance at these divinely inspired events, the atmosphere was special and no one wanted to miss out.

Our American culture doesn't offer anything close to a festival sponsored by God. The events that are the closest to this type of gathering would be the old fashioned camp meetings the Methodists did in yester year, or some of the Promise Keeper weekends the men have attended. And there have been musical Concerts, and Concerts of Prayer that have been festive events that God and His children have enjoyed. But, few gatherings have ever come close to fulfilling the purposes God has in these ordained festivals that He has initiated. Nothing comes close to bringing His family together, children and all the generations in God's forever family around God's Word. Nothing comes close to experiencing the revival, communicating God's ways and imparting identity like these famous feasts.

Each one of the feasts communicates important identity characteristics and the concerns God our Father has for us. In Leviticus Chapter 23 God tells us about these special feasts, He calls them Holy convocations. He reminds us that we are to be Sabbath people; He specifically tells us that we are to be like Him, work for six days and then He requires rest. We are to be just like Him when He created the world. It is interesting note that He has to strongly command us not to work and to be at rest in Him. This is an identity issue with God, we are to be known as people who rest in God and keep the Sabbath rest He commanded in the Ten Commandments.

The writer of the book of Hebrews said, "There remains a Sabbath-rest for the people of God; for anyone who enters God's rest also rests from his own work, Just as God did from his. Let us therefore, make every effort to enter that rest, so that no one will fall by following their example of disobedience" (Hebrews 4:9-10). Our identity is to be seen as obedient children who by faith keep our balance in God by keeping this command to have a Sabbath rest. We are not to be the stressed out people of the world, we are people who find rest in God.

PASSOVER (PESACH)

This Leviticus passage continues to list the feasts God designed to impart to us special identity characteristics. The first is the most famous and the single most important one of all, the Passover. This feast like all of these is to be regarded as a memorial forever (Ex. 12:14). From an identity standpoint we are to be regarded as "Passover People." To help us understand the meaning of the Passover God instructs us to tell and retell the Passover story time and time again. He wants to keep us and our children inspired by this story and draw from it the identity characteristics that He intends from this powerful display of His love as seen in His commitment to His people.

Passover is the Historical story of God miraculously saving His people from brutal slavery in Egypt. Nearly 3500 years ago God's children the Jews were exiled to Egypt and for 400 years they had been suffering as slaves. They were forced to make great structures with hand made bricks for the Pharaoh. He tortured them to produce bricks by the cutting slashes of his brutal taskmaster's leather whips. God's children had strong hands, aching backs and had prospered and maintained great vigor in spite of this oppression. This Passover story is a story about God raising up a deliverer named Moses who gives us a good look at what Jesus is like. He was a man who refused to succumb to the Identity Thief and he decided that he would rather suffer as a child of God than enjoy the cushy life in Pharaoh's palace (Hebrews 11:24).

Moses will always be regarded as a hero. Here we have a Jewish baby who was put into a basket made of tar pitch and placed into the Nile River by his mother; he was then miraculously saved and then raised in Pharaoh's house. He was providentially cared for by his own mother and by God's grace he never forgot his true identity as a child of God. Moses always had a passion for God and His people. In a moment when Moses observed a great injustice, Moses was overcome with righteous indignation and killed an Egyptian who was doing harm to a Jew. This caused Moses to be exiled into the desert of Midian where for forty years God prepared Moses to fulfill his call as Israel's deliverer.

During this preparation period God met Moses in the burning bush and told him that he had heard the cries of his children in Egypt and that He felt their oppression. He told Moses that He wanted to rescue them and bring them out of bondage and into His special land, the promised land of Israel. God then told Moses that He was sending him to stand before Pharaoh and to ask Him to "Let my people go!"

Naturally Moses felt very inadequate for this task, but God reassured him of His presence, His identity and His authority. God supported Moses with his brother Aaron, His name, and his shepherd's staff which became the powerful "rod of God". Moses went back to Egypt as a transformed man, a man who was confident in God's "I Am" identity. Moses is an example to us of a man who takes God's identity, and finds personal confidence and authority in God. Moses went and stood before Pharaoh who is a classic picture of the Identity Thief. Moses and Aaron saw things go from bad to worse, the wicked Pharaoh would make the work conditions worse for God's children by forcing them to make bricks without straw. Yet, Moses and Aaron kept returning and confronting Pharaoh who would attack their identity by calling them names.

God who is the God of truth encouraged Moses by telling him that Pharaoh's heart would be hardened, but that He would show Himself strong by performing miraculous signs and wonders (Ex. 7:3). So, in a made of TV scene Moses, Aaron and the Staff stood before Pharaoh. And at the right time the staff became a snake; this got the Pharaoh's attention. Yet the Pharaoh summoned his sorcerers who in a way replicated this feet, and Pharaoh's heart grew harder.

It seemed futile to ask the Pharaoh to Let God's people go, but after nine creative and costly plagues he relented. These plagues confronted and embarrassed the gods and idols of Egypt and then God pulled off the "Passover." The Passover employed God's trump card, death. In this plague God caused death to move throughout Egypt and kill the first born of everything. But, God's people were protected by the blood of a lamb painted on their door frames and by being under the blood they were saved when death passed over them. God said simply, "I will see the blood and "Passover" them and leave them secure. Even though there was much wailing throughout the land of

Egypt, God's people were kept safe just as He promised. This was a night of great contrast, God's children were praising Him, and the Egyptians were wailing in grief. Finally Pharaoh relented and let God's people go, what an Exodus it was, this was a powerful display of God's commitment to our freedom.

In haste God's children gathered themselves and their possessions and began their march to the Promised Land. In their hurriedness they ate meat roasted over fire, bitter herbs and they didn't have time to let the bread rise. These elements have become the featured items of the Seder Supper God's people have celebrated in remembrance of this Great Passover miracle and exit from bondage.

For the last 3500 years we have been invited to celebrate this Passover meal with the bitter herbs, the unleavened bread and the bone of a lamb to remind us of the Lamb that was sacrificed and how its blood saved God's children. This meal points us to Jesus our sacrificial lamb and deliverer from our bondage to sin. It reminds us how God loves us, responds to our needs, and how powerfully he can cave and deliver us. It is a powerful motivation to be in a constant state of thanksgiving, and the unleavened bread is a reminder to abstain from sin because leaven is seen as sin in the scriptures, and in reality their bondage in Egypt was the result of sin.

Jesus identity required Him to go to Jerusalem on "Lamb Selection Day", to celebrate the Passover. This was His custom, and we feel the thud in His gut as He knew that He would be betrayed, beaten and sacrificed as he was the ordained Lamb of God. He knew what His blood would accomplish; His blood would deliver us from our bondage, just like the blood on the door posts in Egypt cause judgment to "Passover." When His blood is applied to our lives we become secure from identity theft and death and the consequence of our sins will "Passover" all of us who believe. Jesus said, "My time is near; I am to keep the Passover." Jesus overcame the Identity Thief who would try to divert him from the cross, but Jesus overcame Him acting out of His true identity as the Passover Lamb of God. And at 3:00 on that fateful Friday afternoon He died for us at the exact time of sacrifice. Today we who believe in Jesus blood find our value to God in this blood because value is determined by the price that was paid (I

Cor. 3:16). And we overcome the Identity Thief by realizing that Jesus blood shed for us is our testimony (Rev. 12:11), and now our identity is known, we are to be known as blood bought-Passover people.

We who believe in Jesus find our identity in what He has done for us in his suffering and sacrifice. So, we can relate to those bitter herbs (ever taste horse radish all by itself?). and we understand the stripes and the puncture marks on the matzos (unleavened). bread. We behold Jesus like John the Baptist did as the Lamb of God who came to take away the sins of the world. We highly value what happened on that cross of suffering over two thousand years ago; by understanding this truth the Identity Thief can constantly be defeated in our lives. Nothing can diminish the power of the blood as expressed in Jesus death and resurrection for us. By believing this truth we have an indelible identity in Jesus Christ. Peter said, "by His stripes we are healed" (I Peter 2:24)

The Identity Thief has taken this great day and polluted it with bunny rabbits, Easter Eggs and Easter hams for brunch. Have you ever thought of this? Where did the word Easter come from? I challenge you to do your own research, don't just take my word for it, look it up and see for yourself the influence of the Identity Thief.

It must terribly grieve God to see little children reading stories about Easter bunnies when they should be hearing His-story of the Passover. The Identity Thief doesn't want little children to hear of the true Lamb of God, His life, His blood, His death and His resurrection, because when children believe this truth they gain a powerful and sure identity in Jesus.

The Identity Thief took a Pagan god called "Ishtar" and changed the Passover into a pagan laced Easter time void of the blood of Christ and God's faithfulness. This happened because God's people failed to study the scriptures and keep His Passover memorial intact. The Identity Thief has been frauding God of His rightful glory, and defrauding God's children from celebrating this powerful identity imputing feast called the Passover and becoming the thankful people we should be.

THE FEAST OF UNLEAVENED BREAD (Hag HaMatzah)

The next feast God asks us to keep is the feast of Unleavened Bread. This feast is closely aligned with the Passover in time and in story. During the Exodus from Egypt there was such dispatch as God's children paraded out of the land of bondage they didn't have time to wait for the bread dough to rise. God commanded this special feast to commemorate the hasty departure they had from the land of their pain and to remember the consequence of sin (Deut. 16:3, Ex. 12:39)

In talking about this feast God said, "This is a day you are to commemorate; for the generations to come you shall celebrate it as a festival to the LORD—a lasting ordinance. For seven days you are to eat bread made without yeast. On the first day remove the yeast from your houses, for whoever eats anything with yeast in it from the first day through the seventh must be cut off from Israel" (Ex. 12:14-15). It goes without saying that God wanted to communicate some serious identity characteristics with this feast.

There are a couple of powerful identity implications contained in this most unusual feast. To understand the purpose of this feast we need to know that the spiritual meaning of yeast is related to sin. Paul told the Corinthians, "do you not know that a little leaven leavens the whole lump?" (1 Cor. 5:6). The point he is making is that sin corrupts the whole person. The identity issue here is clear, when a person comes to Jesus it is expected that they will take sin seriously and not just consider themselves positionally righteous, but in a practical reality they will seek to purge all the sin out of their lives. For centuries Jews would sweep the leaven out of their homes and be reminded of the "house keeping" we must do to keep our lives pure. We are to have an identity consistent with this level of personal holiness (I John 1:9, 1 Peter 2:9). Paul adds to this thought by saying, "Therefore purge out the old yeast, that you may be a new batch as you really are. Therefore let us keep the festival, not with the old yeast, the yeast of malice and wickedness, but with bread without yeast, the bread of sincerity and truth" (I Cor. 5:7-8)

Paul simply encourages us to live out of our true identity as sincere and truthful people like God (Eph. 5:1). We are people who separate ourselves from sin, and consider holiness to be our normal Christian lifestyle. This feast has many sanctifying identity issues attached to it. Whenever a Jewish child would see their parents going through their house with a feather and a spoon taking great pains to sweep out all the leaven in their home, that child got the picture of how God expects us to keep our lives clean from sin, we are holy people.

THE FEAST OF FIRST FRUITS (Bikkurim)

The Feast of First Fruits is an identity enriching feast. This festival also falls in the springtime during the Passover Week. During this simple celebration God's children are to bring the first ripened sheaf of barley in from the barley field as a First Fruits offering. This festival provides us with an interesting snap shot into history past. Imagine the day when Jesus was arrested, bound and handed over for trial. Remember how the religious leaders were so pious and resolute? It was on this day that these religious leaders of the Sanhedrin would go into the nearby barley fields and bind up a sheaf, yet they would leave the roots attached to the ground to further ripen. Yet this sheaf was bundled so it could be easily cut down and carried. A day later they would return, and harvest it and in joy they would carry it to the temple and present it as their "first fruits" offering. The Apostle Paul saw this snap shot as a very significant picture of Jesus when he said, "But Christ has indeed been raised from the dead, the First Fruits of those who have fallen asleep. For since death came through a man, the resurrection of the dead comes through a man. For as in Adam all die, so in Christ all will be made alive. But each in his own turn; Christ the First Fruits; then when He comes, those who belong to Him" (I Cor. 15:20-22). Do you see the irony of these religious people binding their barley sheaf's to bring an offering to God and in the same day binding Jesus to present Him, He is the true First Fruits, offering, and we being "in Him" become His first Fruits offering to the Father!

His resurrection is the assurance that we too will be raised from the dead. And as a First Fruits offering we will be presented to the Lord. So why wait for the resurrection to experience this new life and to consider ourselves as an offering to the Lord (Romans 12:1-2). This then is a rich feast for us, for not only do we learn the importance of giving to the Lord the first of our produce (Prov. 3:9), but we realize that we are considered the first fruits. The Jews were not allowed to enjoy the produce of the Land until God was satisfied with their First fruits; this is a powerful identity principle. We are people who give the first of everything unto God! We Keep the Lord first! Our identity is that of a giver we give the Lord the first of everything, even our very lives.

THE FEAST OF PENTECOST (Shavout)

We are all familiar with Pentecost, but it is known in the Old Testament as the Feast of Weeks. After seven weeks after the First Fruits were offered in the Temple, the Feast of Weeks was to be celebrated on the Pentecost or the fiftieth day. This feast is also an agriculturally based feast like the first fruits feast, but this represents the first fruits of the summer wheat crop. Even though this is the origin of this special day, this day is now famous for the miraculous things God has accomplished on this day. The Jewish sages believed that it was this day God spoke the Law on Mount Sinai, so this day has become known as the day of the giving of the Torah (Law)

The New Testament significance is that this is the day when the disciples in obedience to Jesus were in Jerusalem waiting for the comforter the Holy Spirit to fall upon them. This day has come to be known as the day of Pentecost. There are similarities to both of these historic days. In both of these Pentecost's God spoke, the wind blew; there was thunder, smoke and fire. These were special days when the Holy Spirit confirmed God the Father's words.

This feast is full of identity significance; it shows how our relationship with the Holy Spirit is the key to understanding who we are in God. Paul said in I Corinthians 2:12, "We have not received the spirit of the world, but the Spirit who is from God, that we may understand what God has freely given us." We are not a lawless and boundary less people, God's Ten Commandments all affirm our identity in Him and in Torah (the first five books of the Old

Testament). And the Holy Spirit enables us to experience an impossible life, a life where Jesus lives His resurrected life in us by the power of the Holy Spirit. Paul said, "Christ in us is the Hope of Glory" (Col. 1:27). The primary purpose of the feast of Pentecost is to affirm this great hope.

These first four feasts are all spring time festivals and in a spiritual way they have been fulfilled in Messiah's first coming. In the next three feasts of Trumpets, Atonement and Booths we will see our identity significance as they relate to Jesus second coming.

THE FEAST OF TRUMPETS (Rosh Hashanah)

The feast of Trumpets, the Day of Atonement and the Feast of Booths are all fall holy days. The feast of Trumpets features the blowing of horns, the ram's horn also called the Shofar, and various other trumpets like the silver trumpet. These horns will be blown in the temple area and all over the country with sounds calling the people to repentance, to awaken, and calls to prayer and to war.

There is a holy fear found in this feast, the fear of not repenting in time of Messiah's coming or in our case in time for His return. Yet because of the nature of this awesome musical sound there is a spirit of celebration in this feast of Trumpets. It is also known as the Jewish New Year or Rosh Hashanah. This is the day when Torah keeping and festival observing people review last years sins both personally and nationally and make apologies for their wrongs. God has made confession, repentance, and the ministry of reconciliation as the natural identity of His people and this feast is intended to impart that DNA.

The blowing of the Trumpets is God's way of awakening His people. No joke! This is exactly His purpose in this feast and in the blowing of the trumpets. The Rabbi's would say, "Awake you sleepers, from your sleep! Rouse yourselves, you slumberers out of your slumber! Examine your deeds, and turn to G-d in repentance. Remember your creator, you who are caught up in the daily round, losing sight of eternal truths, you are wasting your years in vain pursuits that neither profit nor save. Look closely at yourselves;

improve your ways and your deeds. Abandon your evil ways, your unworthy schemes, every one of you" (Yad Hichot Teshuua 3:4)

I have been thinking that this would be a great way to awaken my college age children, I will memorize that rabbinic saying, go into there rooms on a Saturday morning when they are home and bless them with that wonderful recitation, then I will dust off my old coronet (trumpet). and blast reveille. Well, maybe, I won't, seeing my daughter waken in anger is not a pretty sight, my son will just cover his head. And certainly they would not be in any mood to learn the great identity truths I have for them.

In this feast the identity points are clear, God wants to get our attention and He has scheduled the blowing of these trumpets to awaken us. My old basketball coach would yell, be awake, I can still hear his voice. But, can we hear God calling us to be awake? Does your church use the trumpets or remember this ordained day and teach you about the importance of being awake? Does your pastor use this day to remind you to regularly confess your sins and work out your relationships through the cross of Christ?

This feast of Trumpets reminds us that our identity is that of being awake and alive. We are people who are engaged in confession and repentance and we constantly are involved in the ministry of reconciliation, this is who we are. So sound the trumpets and let this glorious sound remind us about who we are, and learn to listen for the trumpet because it just might be the last trumpet announcing our Lord's return for us (1 Corinthians 15:52). This will be a powerful identity affirming day when those who find their identity in Him will meet Him in the air, think about it. Let the trumpet blow, maranatha!

THE DAY OF ATONEMENT (Yom Kippur)

The next feast day Leviticus 23 records is Yom Kippur, the Day of Atonement. This is the most serious and solemn of all the Holy Days. This is the once a year day when the High Priest, the Holy Representative for all the people would reverently and carefully enter the Holy of Holies with in the veil of the temple. He would enter to apply the blood of the Lords goat as a sin offering for the people on the mercy seat. The blood of this sacrifice and this reverent action would hopefully atone, cover, or appease God's anger against them for their sins. This costly and serious act would apply to all the people, the priesthood, and for the nation for the whole year. There was a lot riding on this Day of Atonement.

This entire day is spent fasting and praying, with an attitude of solemn surrender making this "the day" in Israel. And we have great difficulty getting people to come out for a night of prayer, or an early morning prayer service. Leviticus 16:30-31 states, "For it is on this day that atonement will be made for you to cleanse you. Then before the LORD, you will be clean from all your sins. It is a Sabbath of rest, and you must deny yourselves, it is a lasting ordinance."

It is a worthwhile and humbling study to review all the details of this Day of Atonement from the High Priests point of view. This study causes us to see the seriousness of our personal sin and its affect on our nation. It also causes us to get a vivid view of Jesus who is our perfect High Priest who was able to make for us a once for all time atonement and forgiveness of all our sins. The writer of the book of Hebrews explains a New Testament or New Covenant view of the Atonement this way, "Therefore, since we have a great high Priest who has gone through the heavens, Jesus the Son of God, let us hold firmly to the faith we profess. For we do not have a high Priest who is unable to sympathize with our weaknesses, but we have one who has been tempted in everyway, just as we are- yet was without sin. Let us then approach the throne of grace with confidence, so that we may receive mercy and find grace to help us in our time of need" (Hebrews 4:14-16)

This special day has also been called "face to face", for in this Day of Atonement the High Priest would go behind the veil of the temple and at that moment he was "face to face" with the mercy seat of God. He would see a brilliant cloud covering this seat, and experience God's acceptance or rejection of the sacrifices they had previously offered. What I am about to say is the greatest understatement I have ever made. Aren't you glad Jesus is the perfect High Priest whose sacrifice completely satisfies the righteous requirements of our Holy God, so we can now live "face to face" with Him!

God intended for His Day of Atonement to impart to us a Righteous identity, so we can live transparent lives, face to face with God and with each other. This identity and righteous standing enables us to have an identity of confidence as we come before Him in prayer. This confidence that impacts every situation and every relationship we are engaged in, this is who we are (Hebrews 4:16)

THE FEAST OF BOOTHS (Sukkot)

As a boy I loved to attend the Hall county fair, for here I picked up on a real spirit of celebration. The farmers, ranchers, and their families and their hired hands were in the mood to rejoice because their harvest was in the barn and they brought their livestock (animals). to the fair to show and to sell. The hard work was done and now they were going to have something to show for it, they were ready to whoop it up. The festival of booths or Sukkote is the same as this but has so much more.

Deuteronomy 16:13 says, "you shall celebrate the feast of booths seven days after you have gathered in from your threshing floor and your wine vat."

What every young person would love about this week long feast is the camp out experience living in the booths. These temporary dwellings, or huts, or what we would call a tent, created a great camp meeting environment. Can you imagine the fun the children would have camping out with hundred of other children and thousands of friends, and countrymen you long to be with on these annual gatherings. To a child there was some real freedom, adventure and excitement in this festival. And to top it all off the real reason for gathering was to rest, so sleep in, siesta, and lounge around, just hang out with your friends. And think of it, this is what God commanded!

This feast commemorates the days of wilderness wondering after the days of Exodus from Egypt. From a human standpoint these hearty people of God had no business being alive, they could have easily perished in the hot desert, but God miraculously provided for

with David and say, "I was glad when they said "lets go up to the house of the LORD."

IDENTITY IMPARTATION THROUGH GOD'S FEASTS

FEAST	GOD'S IDENTITY	HIS IMPARTED IDENTITY TO US
Passover	Deliverer Prayer Answerer	A Thankful Person A Saved Person. Delivered
Unleavened Bread	Holiness	We Are Sanctified Truth Based Consecrated
First Fruits	Life	We Are Alive We Are Living Sacrifices (Romans 12:1-2)
Pentecost	Lawgiver Spirit	Law Keeping People Holy Spirit Indwelt
Trumpets	Joy Protecting	Repentant Awake and Ready
Atonement	Judge	A Confessing People Forgiven "Face to Face"
Booths	Provider Cloud and Fire	Restful (Sabbath Keeping) Rejoicing Mobile (This Is Not Home)

I believe it is clear, Paul told Timothy, "All Scripture is God-breathed and is useful for teaching, rebuking, correcting and training in righteousness, so that the man of God may be thoroughly equipped for every good work" (2 Timothy 3:16). Try this out and see if a regular study of the Torah, The Ten Commandments and God's feasts will help us go deeper in understanding our identity in God. It is good for us to allow the Word of God to teach us, rebuke us, correct us and train us in righteousness. I encourage all my readers everywhere to give yourselves to this discipline. I guarantee you the Identity Thief hates it when we do, but I think you will agree this study will "rock" our identity and help us find security from identity theft.

Chapter 17
BLUE DEVILED

2 Thessalonians 2:9-13, John 17:17

In March 2006 the TV network news purveyors were telling us a story about the members of the Duke University Men's Lacrosse team. They reported that members of this team ordered a couple of female strippers from an escort service for a team party, they showed up, bared all and then there was a serious outbreak of identity theft. For over a year the name of one of these strippers was kept confidential to protect her identity, because she accused these young men of raping her at the scene of this party. This case was constantly on the news but it took about ten months before the truth started to seep out. This story is a story about massive identity theft because of a blatant disrespect for truth.

Duke University prior to this incident enjoyed a positive reputation. All around our country their fans sported Duke Bluedevil T-shirts and ball caps because they loved their basketball team. This school has been highly respected academically and it has been known as a very expensive and prestigious school. It boasts of educating some of America's best and brightest, so when these "All-American" looking white athletes were accused of gross sex crimes the national media went nuts. Then this story was supercharged when race became an issue. The media was frenzied by the thought of these white boys with the black stripper, and soon this was a story of exploitation and these spoiled rich white boys were pitted against a poor and innocent black woman.

We should all know that it is morally wrong for these young men to hire strippers and feast their eyes on flesh in this way. And it is also wrong for others to excuse this behavior by simply saying, "boys will be boys", this behavior is detestable. These boys should have been taught to wear the crown and find a true and noble identity in Christ and let their behavior flow out of this powerful and holy identity. They should have had a Crown-wearing identity imparted to them by their parents, Pastors and Sunday school teachers, and their coaches. Their participation in pornography whether it is in print, on DVD, the internet, or by ordering a personal strip dancer is one of the Identity Thief's primary ways of degrading people, both men and women, boys and girls. So, regardless how this story was played out these, men and everyone should get the message that porn is shameful and steals identity from both the people who draw pleasure from it, and those who flaunt their bodies. Their planning and participating in this porn party only shows their immaturity and their moral bankruptcy. But, it doesn't make them guilty of the rape charge.

What we witnessed on the evening news was a serious identity theft and a violent assault on the truth. The Durham North Carolina District Attorney (I will not use any names in this story to do my part to prevent identity theft) responded to this story with emotion and a rush to judgment at the expense of the truth. It is very suspicious as to why this DA sided with the striper and said disparaging things in the media about these Duke University Lacrosse players. Some respected TV commentators voiced that he was using this high profile case to promote his own re-election campaign. And he was given a boost by showing his support for this supposed victim, a poor black woman stripper. He made it clear that these rich white boys were not going to walk away from this incident. By his words he was playing the race card and was spinning sexual exploitation to his favor.

In the ensuing days this DA said that he was confident a rape had occurred and called these White Duke Lacrosse players a "bunch of hooligans, whose daddies could buy them expensive lawyers." It didn't help the cause of truth when this DA withheld truthful the DNA records that would have exonerated the players. At the expense of the truth, he conspired with the lab director to withhold this vital information which prolonged these players sense of guilt, and caused them to continue to be the target of derision and disgrace. The players had to hold their heads up in spite of "wanted Posters" that pictured their Lacrosse team and urged the community to come forward with information about this alleged rape. Other students wore t-shirts urging these players to just admit their guilt. And 88 Duke Professors from the Trinity College of Arts and Sciences placed an ad in The Chronicle calling these boys a social disaster and accusing racism and sexism.

Wherever these athletes went they heard the word "rapist" mumbled, and even the Black Panthers came to Durham to taunt them. This Identity Theft was happening right before our national audience; most of the news reports seemed to drip guilt on these Lacrosse Players. In spite of all this identity pain, the DA remained silent, allowing these boys, their families and the school to suffer in silence.

In our court system people are to be considered innocent until they are proven guilty. But, as a result of this DA's lack of care for the truth many identities were maligned. The Duke University was embarrassed on our national stage, their Men's Lacrosse team had to suspend their season, their coach lost his job, some of these young men had to leave this school, and all their families were scorned by the embarrassment of this situation.

The black woman stripper had had her identity damaged before this point in time event. Her disrespect for her own identity is proof that the Identity Thief is the one who raped and pillaged her identity. She promoted herself as "Precious", and I believe this stage name is indicative of the desire of her heart. The scriptures declare (1 Peter 2:4-12) that just as Jesus is precious to God the Father, we too who believe are to be regarded as precious because by faith we are in Jesus. But, the Identity Thief had so victimized this black stripper that he got her to believe that she was worthless. Just as an orange that is squeezed too much loses its value and is thrown into the trash, this is what was happening to this woman. Every time she sexually performed as "precious" she degraded herself. She began to feel so much disgust for herself that she medicated herself with alcohol just to get through these shameful acts.

I believe every person desires to be courted, valued and considered desirable. If only this woman would have constantly been told the truth about God's love for her and her innate value and chose to believe it, this Bluedeviled fiasco would not have happened. If only she would have grown up believing in the God who believes in her, and considers her beautiful and cherishes her. She would have then been able to love herself and respect herself and I believe she never would have stooped to strip before these men. The Identity Thief had so robbed this woman of this hope that now she was turning into an accomplice for the Identity Thief himself. Now it was nothing for her to exploit others, she had been exploited and now she would waylay these men with her words and her actions. All of her doings were consistent with the identity she saw herself wearing. The Identity Thief had imparted to her, his own identity as an accuser. So why are we surprised to hear that she made false accusations, exaggerated the story by saying she had been beaten, strangled, she even tried to get her friend to put marks on her body, and listed several crude forms of vile sex committed against her? She called men out of a line-up who were not even at the party. The Devil is called a liar, and those who follow him behave like he does.

Finally the truth was allowed to shine on this case, and on December 28th 2006 the North Carolina Bar Association filed charges against this District Attorney and his professional misconduct began to surface. It became clear that he had been dishonest and defrauded these young men of proper representation. As a result of good evidence the innocence of these men became clear and the DA would be seen as a deceitful and fraudulent. The DA lost his job and his law license, but the young men, their team and this university had their reputations severely tarnished. And just as you cannot run over a feather pillow with your lawn mower and then retrieve all the feathers and put it back together again, these young men are left with ruined reputations. The courts and the school will hold their hearings and there will be financial settlements to pay for the legal costs and the pain and suffering, but what is an identity really worth?

The reason for telling this story is to show the identity thefts that happen when truth is eroded and trampled on. This story does even more for us; it prepares us for the future. The Bible makes it clear that in the last day's we are going to see truth mocked, and the identities and reputations of people destroyed. It makes it clear that the Identity Thief will be turned loose, his restraints will be lifted and everyone will have their character and identity attacked by him.

The Apostle Paul predicts, "For the secret power of lawlessness is already at work; but the one who now holds it back will continue to do so till he is taken out of the way. And then the lawless one will be revealed, whom the Lord Jesus will overthrow with the breath of His mouth and destroy by the splendor of his coming" (2 Thess. 2:7-8).

The Identity Thief is regarded in scripture as the "lawless one", and we see him at work in the world today. I call him the Identity Thief and we see him working all around the world thru religions, and philosophies bringing people into bondage and under the control of repressive governments or spiritual leaders. The truth is obvious; he has a total disregard for God's laws and the boundaries of good laws in general. To be specific, I believe he has no respect for Torah (the first five books of the Old Testament), or any of the proven principles in the scriptures. Obviously he hates the Gospel and the law of love which is God's perfect way.

We always see God's grace in effect, and up till now this thief is being restrained from causing all the harm he wants to cause. The scripture says we do see him at work, and when ever we see people being oppressed, and controlled we can see this wicked persons footprints that he leaves. But how he is being restrained I really do not know, but I remember God parting the waters and holding them in a heap when Moses led his children through the Red Sea, so I believe God is holding back an onslaught of evil to give us a chance to get right with Him. Because just as the Egyptian army was destroyed when the waters were let loose, when this lawless one is loosed, there will be a tidal wave of evil sweeping over everyone on the earth at that time.

I believe God is using many influences to hold back the evil one at this time. The preaching of the Gospel of Jesus all around the world is bringing about a righteousness that is presently helping to neutralize the evil one. And the identity of His Children themselves makes God jealous to keep us safe, both the Jew's and the Gentile believers in Jesus who now have become Jew's inwardly with circumcised hearts (Romans 2). And of course the Holy Spirit is at work in the world in powerful ways convicting the people of Sin, righteousness and Judgment, (John 16:9) this presence is the most powerful at restraining the Lawless one.

Be encouraged, when this Lawless one is revealed Jesus will return and overthrow him by the breath of His mouth. I believe this is a reference to the authority and power of the Word of God. And we must not forget that it is authoritative and powerful because it is the Word of Truth. The key lesson for us in this study is to know that we are hidden in Christ, His identity and authority has been given to us, and we can appropriate this powerful and securing identity by faith. When we do this we are assured of this awesome victory and it makes us look forward to meeting Him in the air and seeing Him "clean house" and put things back into His divine order here on earth. This is why it is called the splendor of His coming, it is His glorious appearing, and at this moment identity will mean everything. The sheep will be with their shepherd, and the goats will go the way of the Lawless one.

In the story of the Duke Lacrosse players who were defrauded because truth was disregarded, look and see how people will perish in the end days because they refuse to love the truth. The Bible says, "The coming of the lawless one will be in accordance with the work of Satan displayed in all kinds of counterfeit miracles, signs and wonders, and in every sort of evil that deceives those who are perishing. They perish because they refuse to love the truth and so be saved" (2 Thess. 2:9-10). Just as the DA in the Duke case for some intentional reason decided to align himself with the stripper, and seek to defraud these young men, Satan is going to intentionally do the same things, and he will do some very impressive things to deceive and mislead people. His primary tactic is to devalue the truth so that the people will not be protected by it when they are exposed to the counterfeit teachings, miracles, and signs. For sure the battle of the day is the battles for truth, because with out it people cannot be saved.

In verse eleven we will see something that really ticks God off, it is disdain for the truth. And because people intentionally reject the truth, Just like in Romans 1:28 when the people chose their shameful acts over thanking God, and they chose to worship creation rather than the creator the passage says God gave them over into the very sin they were desiring. And men began committing indecent sexual acts with men and women with women. In the end days something similar is going to happen. God Himself is going to send a powerful delusion so that people will believe the lie and be condemned. This is a judgment for the people who have not identified with Jesus and defeated the Identity Thief by placing their faith in Jesus Christ.

The message is very clear; because truth is being maligned today we can know that this Day of Judgment is coming soon. The people who do not believe the truth will be condemned (2 Thess. 2:12) because wickedness is their true identity. But as for us who believe in Jesus Christ, there will be no condemnation, (Romans 8:1) because we have been made into a new creation that is righteous and completely acceptable to God. Just as the Duke Lacrosse players were "bluedeviled", because a striper chose to be a false accuser, and a DA made a rush to judgment and called innocent men guilty because of his failure to appropriate the truth, these last days are going to be a horror picture for everyone who despises the truth. But, those who believe in Jesus, who love the truth and know that their identity is the Righteousness of God in Christ (2 Cor. 5:21), these believers in Jesus can live "no fear", we can be "like a rock", and have constant security from identity theft.

SECURITY FROM IDENTITY THEFT
Study Guides & Discussion Questions for Small Groups

SECTION #1: KNOW IT!

CHAPTER #1: CAN'T STANDS NO MORE

1. What would make Popeye say, "I've had all I can stands and I can't stands no more?" The author says we must take on this attitude and become "Rock-like" to face the Identity Thief. Do you agree or disagree? Why or why not?
2. How can you relate with Karen Lodrick who had her identity stolen by Maria? How does this identity theft story, illustrate spiritual identity theft?
3. In Matthew 7:15 Jesus said, "watch out for false prophets." How is he talking about identity thieves in this text? And how do false prophets play off a person's identity today?
4. What is the Apostle Paul getting us to think about regarding identity theft when he says the devil masquerades as an angel of light? (2 Corinthians 11:14)
5. How can you tell a good tree from a bad tree? Use Matthew 7:16-20 & Galatians 5:22-23 as your standpoint.
6. How is the scripture, "do not judge, or you too will be judged", misused according to the author? (Matthew 7:1)
7. Meditate on Psalm 18:1-3 and Matthew 7:24-27 and write down three reasons you know your life is founded on the rock and you are secure from spiritual identity theft.

Chapter #2: THE JOSEPH STORY

1. Jacob's name means deceiver, how did his son's play a deceptive trick on this trickster?

2. Favoritism didn't help Joseph; do you think the special coat of many colors was a good idea? Yes? no, Why or why not?
3. Joseph had these special dreams as a revelation from God, what would have been a better way for Joseph to communicate his identity to others?
4. Can you think of any significant Bible character that did not experience rejection? If so who?
5. Even Jesus had to experience rejection? Why? How did Joseph's rejection give us a glimpse into the life of Jesus? (John 1:12)
6. How did Joseph's understanding of his true identity help him deal with Mrs. Potaphar?
7. In your opinion how did Joseph's prison sentence and false accusations against him impact his faith, character and identity?
8. How did God use Joseph's prison experience to make him "rock-like"?
9. Would you have played deceptive games with Joseph's brothers if you were Joseph? Yes? No? Why or why not?
10. How do you see Joseph wearing the crown? Physically? And spiritually? (discuss)

Chapter #3: DILUTED MAN

1. How can a person identify with Jesus and not integrate Jesus into their own life? (1 Corinthians 3:1-4)
2. How did the lack of discipleship/mentoring contribute to Stu's loose gravel like life?
3. How did Stu's addiction to pornography bring about his wash-out? How did God use this crisis to help him find his life and true identity in Jesus? (James 1:13-25)
4. If you were dating and considering marriage what level of health would you need in your own life to be able to make this life time commitment? In your partners? How did Stu fail to understand this in his life and in Kathy's?

5. When the author says, "Stu had to learn about wearing the crown the hard way", what does the author mean?
6. Stu had a habit of going to porn to get "his needs met", how could a proper understanding of his identity in Jesus have kept him out of this sin box? What are some practical ways of escape? (1 Corinthians 10:13)
7. How did the girls at the strip clubs give Stu a false sense of intimacy and inflate his ego?
8. How has the Identity Thief tried to give Stu some negative names? List three of these and discuss.
9. Discuss the price Stu has had to pay? To you what has been the most costly loss?
10. According to Philippians 2:1-5 how should a man lay down his life for his wife? How does a Christ like identity make this difference?
11. Review the Pyramid to Victory in the Appendix. See the steps that lead to self control. What is your sticking point?

Chapter #4: BE A MENORAH

1. Why is it so difficult for us to grasp darkness? Why does this truth make light so meaningful?
2. Explain the correlation between Jesus the "light of the world" and the menorah.
3. By looking at the diagram of the menorah explain its significance. And the story.
4. Why do you believe the Menorah Candles were replaced by a Christmas tree? Or was it?
5. The author says the more we become like Jesus the more Jewish we will look and act. What do you think of that comment?
6. How does this history lesson about Mattathias and his son's revolt against Antiochus impact your faith?
7. Do you think there is to be a correlation between the earthly temple in Jerusalem and your heart as the temple of the Holy Spirit? (I Corinthians 3:16)

8. Why does the author relate the oil to the Holy Spirit?
9. Why would this Menorah remind Jesus that He would have a time of suffering in Gethsemane?
10. Why is it important for us to see our identity in the Menorah as true Jews? (Romans 2:17-29)

SECTION #2, "NAME-IT!"

Chapter#5: LIKE A ROCK STAR

1. According to 2 Corinthians 5:17, how can a Rock star like Alice Cooper have the identity of a new creature in Christ?
2. How does Bob Seger's song LIKE A ROCK, parallel the life of King David? Give three parallels.
3. When David took the challenge to fight Goliath—what identity issues did he have to confront to be able to put this giant in his place? List three (I Samuel 17-18)
4. Read Psalm 23 and identify five ways David found his identity in God as a Shepherd.
5. The song the women sang and danced to about Saul killing his thousands and David killing his ten-thousands, how did this become a serious identity issue for Saul? And for David?
6. David wrote a great "rock" song in Psalm 18—what are your favorite lyrics? And how is it that he relates to God as a rock? List five ways.
7. How did David's rejoicing in god about the Ark being returned to Jerusalem prove to be an embarrassment to his wife? And what identity principle can we learn from David in this experience?
8. How did King David allow himself to sin with Bathsheba? How could he have prevented this by constantly reinforcing his understanding of his identity in God?
9. How did David try to cover his sin with an identity theft?
10. Read Psalm 51 and determine the impact of God's mercy on restoring David's sense of identity.

11. In Psalm 40, 61, and 27 we read David's lyrics—would he be a rock star today? How do these songs encourage you to be like a rock?

Chapter #6: GREAT FAKE OUTS

1. For Pistol Pete to set up one of his patented basketball jump shots he used some fake outs, discuss a typical physical move he would use to pull this off (What are three types of fakes?). Now, relate these fakes to the fake outs the identity uses in the spiritual realm of life.
2. How was Pete disheartened by having his own identity being labeled as the "Pistol"?
3. How did his dad (Press). contribute to Pete's identity struggle?
4. Why did Pete look to Eastern mysticism, Yoga, Vegetarianism, and even microbiotics? Could these searches have been his search for identity?
5. Just as Pete had a great ability to keep his eye on the rim how can we keep our eye on our spiritual goal and protect ourselves from identity theft?
6. The Identity Thief's first fake out is the hard packed heart. Explain how did this fake out describe Coach Tate Almond?
7. The Identity Thief's second fake out is the rocky heart; explain how does the Rocky Nameth story describe this fake out move?
8. The third fake out move is also a fake conversion. What is meant by the terms true and false conversion? How does the Dustin Timberlake story explain these?
9. The author says he no longer tells people that they are going to heaven because they said a prayer. Based on Romans 8:16 do you agree or disagree with this approach?
10. Bank tellers study real money and not fake money to know what true money is. How does this approach apply to the problem of spiritual fake outs?

Chapter #7: GOD'S JEHOVAH NAMES

1. What do you think the author means with his "three things we need to know about God" approach?
2. Why is it that some children don't really know their father, or want to know their father? How does this apply to the spiritual side of life?
3. What does the name "I Am", mean?
4. What does the name Jehovah-Jireh mean? From what story do we get this name? (Genesis 22:14)
5. What does the name Jehovah-Rophe mean? From what story do we get this name? (Exodus 15:26)
6. What does the name Jehovah-Nissi mean? From what story do we get this name? (Exodus 17:15)
7. What does the name Jehovah-Mekeddeshem mean? From what story do we get this name? (Leviticus 20:7-8)
8. What does the name Jehovah-Shalom mean? From what story do we get this name? (Judges 6:24)
9. What does the name Jehovah-Rohi mean? From what story do we get this name? (Psalm 23)
10. What does the name Jehovah Shammah mean? From what story do we get this name? (Exodus 48:35)
11. What does the name Jehovah-Tsidkenu mean? From what story do we get this name? (Jeremiah 23:6)
12. Who is Jehovah-Savior? From what story do we get this name? (John 3:16)
13. The author gives a practical way for God to become bigger to us, what is this method? In your opinion how does knowing God in His Jehovah names strengthen your identity in Him?

Chapter #8: RESPECT OUR ROOT

1. Why is respect such an important aspect when we consider unity?

2. Why do some Christians see themselves as Gentile-believers? In your opinion is this acceptable? (Romans 2:17-29)
3. What are some Jewish symbols that might be confusing to you? List them and discuss (by studying them we can grow to appreciate them more)
4. Why do you think there is Jew hate (anti-Semitism). in the world today? What can we do to change this situation? How can respect for our root transform this landscape?
5. Why do we need to have a "grace" basis to promote respect and unity?
6. How is it by grace that we are "grafted" in? What does this mean according to Romans 11:18?
7. How can respect and unity be the answer to Jesus prayer in John 17?
8. Is there any good reason for a Believer in Jesus to live like a Gentile?
9. What are the two people groups in the world today?
10. How do our western ideas about independence hinder our hopes for unity in the Olive tree?
11. Discuss the Acrostic RESPECT, and list what each letter means.
12. Of the seven practical ways the author lists to show respect to the root, which ones are you going to do? What other ones should be added to this list?

Chapter #9: OWN YOUR GOOD NAME

1. What impact did Sid's Grandpa's tragic accident have on Sid's feeling about his identity?
2. By drawing our identity from God our Father, how does this negate a bad or a good earthly family history?
3. What was Sid's attitude towards his step grand mother who saw herself as a "blueblood"? What should it have been?
4. Discuss the nickname stories. Why do you think Jesus gave out nick names?

5. Can we pick our own name? In a spiritual way can we pick our own name? (Proverbs 22:1)
6. Discuss Peter's old address, and now his new one (1 Peter 1:3-5, 2 Peter 1:1-2)
7. What are some practical things we can do to own our good name? (Start now by enjoying a time of giving thanks to God for your good name. Psalm 100:4)
8. How does knowing Jesus level the playing field when it comes to identity? (Isaiah 61:1-5)
9. How is taking care of your good name your primary business? Discuss the Weyerhaeuser, Ford, Firestone and Enron stories.)
10. According to Psalm 23 what does our Good Shepherd do to own His good name?

Section #3: ENGRAVE IT!

Chapter #10:BADGES, LANYARDS, UNIFORMS AND TRAMP STAMPS

1. What lessons about identity can we learn from J.D. "Buck" Savage the crime fighter?
2. According to Matthew 20:26-28 what would be the true symbols of a servant?
3. The author uses the acrostic CARE –discuss the meaning of each letter. Do you agree with this CARE approach to service? Why or why not?
4. Why does the author think "Strings" or lanyards can be symbols that contribute to disrespect?
5. How can a person's job cause identity confusion? What is the plus side of "strings"? And what is the down side from an identity standpoint?
6. What approaches must we take toward "Strings" to avoid identity theft?

7. How can a uniform transform someone's attitude for good, and for bad?
8. Do you think the author is out of line in talking about "Tramp stamps"? Why or why not?
9. According to John 13:34-35 what is the real mark of a Christian?
10. How can we have this mark engraved on our hearts?

Chapter#11: THE MARK

1. How does the author relate the Dr. Seuss Star Bellies, to circumcision? Can you see this parallel? Yes? No? Why or why not?
2. According to Genesis 17:12-14 why was circumcision given by God as a covenant? What do you think God's motive was here? (List at least three ideas)
3. In 1 Peter 3:3-4 Peter wrote about women and told them not to find their identity in the external accoutrements. Why?
4. According to Romans 2:25-29 what circumcision has value?
5. How was the Apostle Paul once a Religious person before his heart was circumcised?
6. According to Deuteronomy 30:6 how do our hearts get circumcised? And what happens to our relationship with god after this "surgery"?
7. How does heart circumcision contribute to unity and the "one new man" of Ephesians 2:11?
8. By using the Grace River Illustration-what must the people do on each side of the river, if they are going to be in the River of God's Grace together?
9. How do the "6Ps" hinder unity?
10. How does a circumcised heart give us a heart of gratitude? How does this contribute to unity?

Chapter #12: COVENANT IDENTITY

1. What was Susie Brown looking for in a marriage covenant, regarding her identity?
2. How can people use covenants, wills and contracts to try and find a basis for their identity?
3. Discuss a couple of God's conditional covenants and ask, "if we do what? What will God do in return"?
4. What covenant imparts to us a perpetually positive identity? (Hebrews 8:6-13)
5. How are the Mosiac (Moses). Covenants (Ten Commandments). conditional covenants? (list five of these by stating the condition and then list the promise)
6. According to genesis 9:9-13 how can a rainbow be a positive identity enhancer? How can this symbol be a reminder of God's grace?
7. List a couple of Old Testament covenants that point us to Jesus and the New Covenant (2 Samuel 7:14-16, Deuteronomy 11:29, 27:12, Genesis 9:9-13)
8. How is the New Covenant a better covenant? (list three ways, Hebrews 8:6-8)
9. List five of God's attributes and state how these identity traits can help to make us secure?
10. List your favorite seven of the Thirty Three Covenant Benefits, and state why these are your seven.

Chapter #13: IDENTITY IN COMMUNION

1. How does Jesus impart His identity to us in the sacrament of Communion? (List three ways)
2. List three names for the Lord's Supper. Discuss the reason for the elements? Why the bread? Why the wine or the grape juice?
3. Why did Jesus use bread to relate with us physically?

4. Why did Jesus use the wine to refer to the blood of the New Covenant?
5. Why did the devil tempt Jesus to turn stones to bread? What is the identity lesson here? (Matthew 4:4)
6. Walk with Jesus to the cross, how did Jesus suffer for us? (List seven ways). According to 1 Peter 2:20-21 how are we to identify with Jesus?
7. How does saying thanks to God-help us enter into our identity in Him?
8. How was the Blood and the cross God's way of satisfying His holiness? (Keeping to His own identity)
9. Why did Jesus have to become sin? (2 Corinthians 5:21)
10. How was Michael's story a story about a young man finding his security in Jesus identity?

SECTION #4: ROCK-IT!

Chapter #14: THE ATTRIBUTES OF GOD"ROCK" OUR IDENTITY

1. Compare the joy of driving a new car, to the joy of getting to know who God really is!
2. What are the attributes of God? (What does the word attribute mean?)
3. How can God's attributes change our thinking about God? How can knowing these qualities about God enhance our own identity?
4. According to Romans 1:20-25 how can our thinking about God become futile? How can thinking through these attributes save us?
5. Why does the author think this study of the Attributes of God will result in praise and worship?
6. What is your favorite Moral-attribute of God? (list the Moral Attributes)

7. What are your two favorite Non-Moral Attributes of God?

8. How can you use this study and meditating on God's Attributes to deal with your own identity issues? (name your issue, you don't have to write it down, but do be serious about it)

Chapter #15: GOD'S PURPOSES FOR HIS LAWS

1. What influences did the Identity Thief use to dissuade David?
2. In your opinion why does hypocrisy have such a negative impact on people?
3. How did a rules basis prompt David to rebel?
4. What did God say to introduce His Ten Commandments with a grace emphasis? (Exodus 20)
5. What is the role of the Holy Spirit in helping us to obey God's laws? Commandments? (Romans 7-8)
6. What Commandments of the famous Ten pertain to our relationship with God? Which ones pertain to our relationships with others?
7. Without looking at the Bible text list the Ten Commandments. How many can you write down? Why do you think these commandments get so overlooked today in our society?

Chapter #16: GOD'S FEASTS

1. How are God's feasts a glad and happy experience? What do these tell us about God's identity? (Psalm 122:1)
2. According to the Parable of the Prodigal Son in Luke 15 what are the identity imparting gifts the father gave to the prodigal son? (list them, and their spiritual significance)
3. Knowing that God loves feasts and festivals, what does this tell you about God's will for your life?

4. How does the Sabbath-rest communicate to us about our identity? (Hebrews 4:9-10)
5. What are we to learn about our identity in the Passover?
6. What are we to learn about our identity in the Feast of Unleavened Bread?
7. What are we to learn about our identity in the Feast of First fruits?
8. What are we to learn about our identity in the Feast of Pentecost?
9. What are we to learn about our identity in the Feast of Trumpets?
10. What are we to learn about our identity in the Day of Atonement celebration?
11. What are we to learn about our identity in the Feast of Booth's?
12. How does the "All Scripture" principle of 2 Timothy 3:16 apply to learning about our identity in god through these special feasts?

Chapter #17: BLUEDEVILED

1. How is the Duke Blue devils Lacrosse Team Story of 2006 a story about a massive identity theft?
2. How were the young men failing to live their identity out of the Crown? (review what the CROWN means, go over each letters meaning)
3. How did the Durham North Carolina DA (District Attorney). commit identity theft? (List three ways)
4. How was the sacrifice of truth the cause of these identity thefts?
5. How had the black female stripper had her identity stolen even before this event? What kinds of things did she do to mask (cover). her personal pain?
6. According to 2 Thessalonians 2:7-8 what Identity Thefts will we see in the future? In your opinion how will these be accomplished?

7. Why does the Identity Thief hate God's Laws, and truth?
8. What is God using to hold back the tidal wave of evil that is in the world today? (list three things)
9. How will Christ's return be the ultimate identity test?
10. How do you know that you have security from identity theft? What role does truth play in your confidence?

Notes and Recommended Reading List:

The Vanishing Conscience, John E. MacArthur Jr., 1994, Word Publishing, Dallas, TX.

Our Father Abraham, Marvin R. Wilson, 1989, Wm. B. Eerdmans Publishing Co., Grand Rapids, MI.

The Messianic Church Arising, Dr. Robert D. Heidler, 2006, Glory of Zion International Ministries, Denton, TX

The Adversary, Mark I Bubeck, 1975, Moody Press, Chicago IL.

God's Grace To You, Charles Haddon Spurgeon , 1997, Whitaker House, New Kensington, PA.

How People Grow, Dr. Henry Cloud, Dr. John Townsend, 2001, Zondervan, Grand Rapids, MI.

The Seven Festivals of the Messiah, Edward Chumney, 1994, Treasure House, Shippensburg, PA.

Restoration, D. Thomas Lancaster, 2005, Fruits of Zion, Inc., Littleton, CO

Feasts of the Lord, Ron Cantrell, Israel.

Our Hebrew Connection, Nancy Byram and Becky Preble, Hebrew Connection Ministries, (ourhebrewconneciton.com), San Antonio, TX.

The Unusual Suspect, Stephen Baldwin and Mark Tabb, 2006, Warner Faith, New York.

Appendix 1

As we grow in love the fruit naturally appears!
Like a tree - we abide in the vine and the SAP flows! John 15:5-8

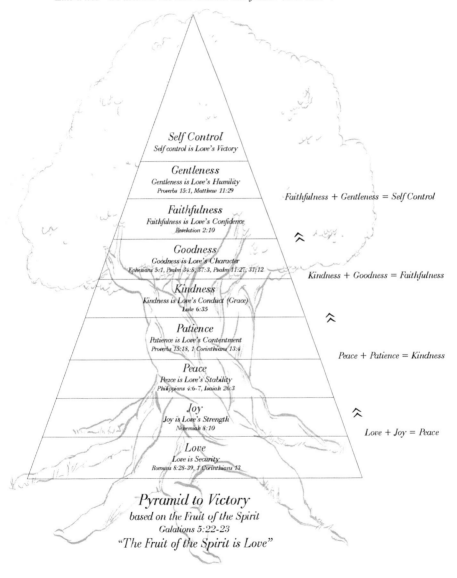

Self Control
Self control is Love's Victory

Gentleness
Gentleness is Love's Humility
Proverbs 15:1, Matthew 11:29

Faithfulness
Faithfulness is Love's Confidence
Revelation 2:10

Goodness
Goodness is Love's Character
Ephesians 5:1, Psalm 34:8, 37:3, Psalm 11:27, 31;12

Kindness
Kindness is Love's Conduct (Grace)
Luke 6:35

Patience
Patience is Love's Contentment
Proverbs 15:18, 1 Corinthians 13:4

Peace
Peace is Love's Stability
Philippians 4:6-7, Isaiah 26:3

Joy
Joy is Love's Strength
Nehemiah 8:10

Love
Love is Security
Romans 8:28-39, 1 Corinthians 13

Faithfulness + Gentleness = Self Control

Kindness + Goodness = Faithfulness

Peace + Patience = Kindness

Love + Joy = Peace

Pyramid to Victory
based on the Fruit of the Spirit
Galatians 5:22-23
"The Fruit of the Spirit is Love"

Appendix 2
The Grace River Model

The Word is Truth
God's Law/Ten Commandments
All Truth including science/history

Prayer

MT. Truth

Fellowship

Bible Study

The Truth side shows God's sovereignty

Worship

Service

Stewardship

Life

Love

The Banks of

Discipline

Peace

The Discipline side shows our
human responsibility

Purpose

Power

True Identity

Blessings

Life in
Grace River.
The Spirit
Controlled Life

Sid Huston Media

CrownScepter316

Identity, Authority & the Good News

CrownScepter316 exists to present Bible-based teaching and proclaim the message of the kingdom of God. The logo of the Lamb with the Scepter and the Crown communicates our call to help people discover their identity in Jesus Christ through His kingly Crown. The letters of the word CROWN capture the meaning of identity: Christ, Righteousness, Order, Worship and Nobility. The Scepter has always stood for the King's authority, which is the Word of God. The 316 is in reference to the good-news passage in John 3:16 which tells the world of God's Love, Jesus' sacrifice, and

Sid Huston Media the life that is available to all who believe. This purpose is to be fulfilled through writing, preaching, public speaking, comedy, radio, and the development of transferable materials. This service also exists to train and involve new workers for the end time's harvest.

The "Who's Your Daddy? Forum

Sid is presently working on pamphlets and seminars that will help explain the identity thefts present in the major religions and cults in the world. In these Forums, he will show the lives of the religious leaders the Identity Thief has distorted, and he will expose the lies the various religious leaders have introduced to the world. This Forum uses the *Security From Identity Theft* model as the basis for discussion. You may contact Sid at Sidhuston@msn.com to inquire.

To schedule a speaking engagement, contact the author at
SidHuston@msn.com

Dr. Vernon Grounds, Chancellor of Denver Seminary, says, "Grace River Living is a treasure house of truth and inspiration."

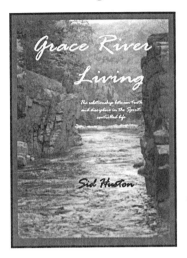

Grace River Living

*Thoroughly biblical, theologically sound, and filled with practical help and revealing anecdotal stories, **Grace River Living** will become your companion as you seek joy, love, encouragement, laughter, growth, peace, forgiveness, release, and trust in Jesus' promise for the abundant life.*

Five beautiful, substantive, and encouraging themes flow from Grace River Living:

In *Picture of Grace River* you will capture an inspiring vision of Grace River and learn how God's grace can captivate you.

In *Mount Truth* you will discover the ageless majesty and precious stability that forms the basis for thinking that will transform your life.

In *The Bank of Discipline* you will see how to work with the Holy Spirit to build your life on the Rock. You will see how inward and outward disciplines (emotionally healthful practices)are practical ways to experience God more fully.

In *The Power of Water* you will learn to recognize and gain respect for a life lived in Grace River and begin to see how this river can flow through you.

In *Stay in Grace River* you will become confident in God's power and commitment to keep you standing in the stream of grace for a lifetime.

To Purchase: Call **800-266-0999** and ask for *Grace River Living*

Coming Soon from Sid Huston Media:

Security from Identity Theft
Book #3
"Be Light!"

This book dives into some of the tough issues men and women face like alcoholism, pornography and eating disorders. It focuses on the securing power of God's love and gives many practical insights into securing your conscience and your self-image. This book contains a "light shield" and a *bonus section*, a very easy to use **Identity Counseling Model** that will help you better understand yourself and help a friend.

Security from Identity Theft
Book #4
"All We Need to Know"
This book is a running commentary on the book of 1 John. This resource will give you Biblical insights into security from identity theft. Four sections: cogitate, contemplate, appropriate, and celebrate! Inspiring truths that will help us believe right, live right and take flight! Read it and see how knowing Jesus is all we need to know. Complete with study guide and discussion questions..

Reserve your copies in advance. Order Today!
Call 800-266-0999 for shipment as soon as these fine books are off the press!